C000001624

The Seven Ss
All the Ss To Your Successes

A Compendium Guide to Management Knowledge

by
Paul Fitzsimmons

Grosvenor House
Publishing Limited

This book is published by
Grosvenor House Publishing Ltd
Link House
140 The Broadway, Tolworth, Surrey, KT6 7HT.
www.grosvenorhousepublishing.co.uk

A CIP record for this book
is available from the British Library

ISBN 978-1-83975-029-8

Images by
Burnett Design Ltd. The Old Coach House,
Yard 143 Stricklandgate Kendal, Cumbria LA9 4RF
T: 07551 166 120 W: neilburnett.co.uk

SELF strong surprising splendid
splendiferous structure success self-worth self-discipline
sell STAFF sight sound smell senses smart
sixfold seize suffix sequence simultaneous
swanky STANDARDS supply spectacular
steady sufficient succinct sociable SIMPLY
sumptuous smile sweetness sacred superior
swift special safety special STOCK synergy
satisfied self-esteem soulful secure satisfied
SERENDIPITOUS SERVICE LEVELS surrogate
solutions systematic synergy support stealth
synonymous SALES Symbolise scented
salubrious sacred satisfaction salvation
SHRINKAGE saintly scrumptious seamless
SELFLESS sensational superb sensuous
sensible significant SKILLED smooth
sophisticated stretching spontaneous swift speedy
sportsmanlike stable SERVICE sensibility

To

My good friend Freddy

Happy New Year

Paul

Contents

Foreword

Put up or shut up. That's what they say. If you have something to say, say it. You don't have to sit in silence. If what you have to say has value, people will listen. Growing up as the youngest of four, I felt I always had something to say, or maybe I felt I had to say something! So I have always done just that. Say what is on my mind. This can obviously make one seem very opinionated, but it seems such a waste to lock away knowledge and not pass on what we have learnt. Knowledge can come absolutely free or it can come at a price. That price can be monetary, timely or emotionally, but it is still knowledge gained and how one acquired it becomes secondary. It is what we do with that knowledge that is important. Keep it, hide it or share it. Later in life, as a manager, I learnt that I wanted to share it and, with more than twenty-five years in the management game, after doing it, trying it, studying it and finally teaching it, I thought it time to share it with a wider audience.

In our youth we seem to not want to know. We seem to know everything and refuse to be told. We do not want to listen. Then as we mature we are more prepared to listen and want as much as we can, constantly researching and asking our elders to hand it over. Then finally, later in life, it seems we just want to get rid of it and pass it on. As a young boy I was lucky enough to get to spend many quality hours tinkering with motor-bikes, engines and so on in the garage with my father. As a young boy I learnt so much from him, but as I grew older I decided that I knew best and stopped listening to him. Here I've always enjoyed the anecdote that suggests: *"When I was seven I was amazed by how much my father knew. When I was seventeen I was disappointed by how little he knew. When I reached twenty-seven I was amazed by how much he had learnt in the last 10 years!"*

Back in the late '70s, as a sixteen-year-old Saturday lad working in my local supermarket, I remember the managers in their flamboyant shirts and ties, giving out instructions and advice. Of course in those days I was never involved in such conversations with them. That was not the way back then. You only spoke when you were spoken to and only said good morning, to what seemed to me, very important people at the time. Little did I know that I would later join their ranks as a would-be aspiring young manager?

I joined my first PLC Company in the early '90s. Unbeknown to me at that time, the UK was beginning yet another great shift in corporate culture. Having only known military life, I knew little about customer service or retailing or indeed managing in a commercial field. I had learnt only to clean and stack shelves and run errands on a Saturday.

Going straight into the forces after school, my life revolved around commands and orders with hard discipline. Boy, did I have some learning to do. After leaving the services I started at the bottom as a warehouse department manager with a large national DIY chain. I will never forget the inspiration I felt when that company sent its entire workforce off to a customer service seminar. We were going all American and I was enthralled. Engrossed, I found the presentation both motivational and inspirational and for me it was a 'eureka' moment where I decided there and then that this was a path I wished to follow. I was lucky, as the firm I was working for at the time was going through a huge cultural shift and my learning and understanding came about from being part of that cultural change and, for me, only reinforced my decision of career path. As I set out on my journey, this open-minded and cultural shift within the company supported me hugely and my contract of employment with my firm truly became a two-way street.

Acknowledgements

I thank my amazing, loving partner for her relentless and unwavering support and belief.

I thank my parents and the armed forces for my first lessons in management, and the 'School of Life' for the rest.

Paul Fitzsimmons

> *"A child educated only at school is an uneducated child."*

George Santayana, novelist and philosopher

Introduction

As a manager, supervisor, co-ordinator, junior manager, area manager or team leader, we will be running or helping to run some type of business model or assisting in the organisation of people. The application of 'the Seven Ss' has a logical order and place of priority. Most businesses nowadays run on automated EPOS (electronic point of sale or barcodes) computerised systems and, therefore, have a perpetual cycle of points, each point relying on the previous point to make up the cycle, like cogs in the proverbial machine. 'The Seven Ss' follow a similar path or flow in a cyclonic direction to achieve their goals and support the next phase of the cycle. To help us see the priorities and understand how we can improve how we see our role, here they are laid out in stages and, like an EPOS system, once installed and established, become an integrated, perpetual and cyclic approach with no real start point, but with all points relying integrally on one another: self, staff, standards, stock, sales, shrinkage and service. If we imagine a circle with these headings as pointers, or that of a clock dial, we can see the rotation of the clock hand ticking past these headings perpetually, moving on from one to the other.

You may not be familiar with 'the Seven Ss', but you may be familiar with the TV programme *Gordon*

Ramsay's Kitchen Nightmares or maybe you have seen Alex Polizzi (granddaughter of the late Charles Forte of the Posthouse Forte hotel group) as *The Hotel Inspector*. In these programmes, the TV celebs enter into struggling business establishments and set about putting things right. In the process and for the benefit of good TV viewing, they stick to a format. The format is a similar approach to the Seven Ss, although they do not label it or format it precisely. Firstly they set about understanding the owners or proprietors of the failing restaurants or hotels. Once they have a working understanding of the owners they then focus their attention on the problems of the businesses. They then move through the problems such as the poor food, dirty bedrooms or unreliable staff. Once the TV celebrities get the owners to understand and see what they see, they begin to reinvent and turn around those problems to improve and rebuild the business. This celebrity approach does help the failing business turn around, but I do not believe guarantees complete success, as the core values and basic skills required need to be fully embedded and cemented into the teams to instil them as foundations and building blocks for the long term by strong coaching and training. Of course, much of the programme is for TV entertainment purposes and we would always expect to see a positive result from these sixty minute makeovers.

After many years in management, moving up the ranks from branch to branch, depot to depot, area to area, and company to company and after building up my own group of companies also (without any celebrity assistance!) I slowly began developing a system that I could see was repeating itself over and over. The rules of engagement became much the same wherever I went and it became clear there was a pattern. I had developed a pattern that seemed to work in order to achieve my objectives and over the course of time it became more structured. This pattern became 'the Seven Ss'. Initially, as I began to write down my methods to help me put some structure into my approach, it was purely by coincidence that the topics and subjects I adopted seemed to constantly fall under the letter S. As I researched and developed the system more it became clear that the letter S really did support many, many superb (see?) positive words, adjectives, verbs and acronyms. Each time I wanted to brand or describe something, I found things coincidentally beginning with the letter S. I found this approach helpful and fun and it enabled me teach it to teams and get staff on board far easier with what I was trying to achieve. This in turn made my teaching easier and, therefore, quicker, which gave me faster turnarounds and swift (see?) performance success (see?).

Although very watchable, the TV examples were just that, TV. Unlike 'the Seven Ss', the programmes fail to cement and totally embed into the process long-term habits and cultures. The aim of my approach and by using this book, I believe, is far more personal and really asks readers (learners) to immerse themselves into developing and understanding themselves first, then view the management process holistically with a firm structure and then see the bigger picture as a perpetual, cyclic process. However, before we try to change the world it is important to understand that none of us are perfect and as managers we must first truly and honestly try to understand ourselves and our abilities. Then we can begin to understand others. "Seek first to understand, and then be understood."

Prevention really is better than cure and in the wake of the digital age technology is affecting the very fabric of our traditional marketplace. This decade has seen declining shop numbers, national chain store closures and not just high street premises, but also retail park buildings becoming redundant. This pressure has also been felt by estate agencies, banks, pubs, filling stations and corner shops. With the likes of Amazon and eBay on the march, online suppliers (now even supermarkets) seem unstoppable. Online retailers are forever developing their offer and, tied with higher trading standards laws, great online service is outpacing old-fashioned high street service. Argos Online in the UK has been so focused on service that they have won awards and prestige for next-day deliveries. I have even ordered a large HD TV online myself Saturday evening to have it delivered before 10 o'clock the next morning! This level of service is unprecedented and far superior to high street offers. The likes of Amazon Prime and online free deliveries all force the high street outlets to compete with themselves and buying online is now a more rewarding experience reinforced by 'likes, feedback, offers' and, of course, Trustpilot. All this should reinforce the point, to improve the service we offer in our traditional businesses. Similarly, technology is replacing management in factories and processing plants too, collating, analysing and redistributing information and spitting out logarithms and algorithms, running simulations and bypassing many traditional management roles. Perhaps, then, now has never been a more important time to flex what management muscle we have left to help us achieve traditional sales goals.

So then, as managers, new or experienced, we must be proactive to combat or at least stay in step with this new phenomenon. Having a prepared and planned approach to maintaining sales and service is crucial to any businesses and to that end retaining traditional customers is clearly absolutely vital. Even moving with this digital tide into faceless online commerce systems, managers of tomorrow should also, then, have a planned approach needed to help manage the unstoppable onslaught of twenty-four hour, next-day delivery, push button, drop into basket, press enter, online shopping and electronic management. I firmly believe that if we choose to follow the Seven Ss structure we will surely begin to develop ourselves with this system as a support function. We will improve our work and, therefore, our performance safely, within a framework, to our daily and weekly activities and responsibilities.

The 7 Ss to Your Successes

The Seven Ss

"There are known knowns. These are things we know that we know. There are known unknowns. That is to say, there are things that we know we don't know. But there are also unknown unknowns. There are things that we don't know we don't know."

Donald Rumsfeld, former US Secretary of Defence

Objectives

I initially intended to part with this knowledge for the benefit of the more junior and upward-coming managers, but, nearing completion of the book, I felt, as with most books of its kind, it is certainly worth a look. I would urge anyone, manager or not, to at least have a read, but especially senior managers of area, regional and director status too, for we are all always learning and do not know everything. A lot of its contents may be absolute common sense to the more experienced, but if we are honest with ourselves there may be things that we knew, but did not know we knew, or even forgot we knew. To others it could just be a prompt or nudge to remind us to step back on to the path, as life's busy and turbulent weather has pushed us off course. Even if we are not managers I believe this book can help others and just allow folk to say 'I might try that or have a look at that', as most of its rules laid out apply to everyday life, both at work and in domestic scenarios too.

I have always believed in value for money (VFM) and, to that end, I urge all readers to get the very most out of this book. Circle words and phrases, highlight, red pen, asterisk, mark up, challenge and question statements and its facts and research items from the book to simply benefit and develop one self. I still do this to this very day, as learning is a lifetime of work. This book (which I hope you enjoy and keep in a desk or drawer handy for reference) is just to say: "Hey, look! We know how tough it can be out there, trying to climb those corporate ladders and those 'greasy' poles." It can be a real struggle trying to get yourself noticed, to better yourself and find the next promotion to improve your role and income and, therefore, your life and your general well-being. Generally this is what most of us want. But we all need some inspiration sometimes too. We all need a mental detox from time to time and some reinvigoration. This book simply aims to point out some of the 'obvious' things that at times may not be quite so obvious. Some of this book's contents may be familiar and other items may be new. Common sense is not always quite common sense until it is learnt and can often require paradigm shifts. You have to understand it, teach it or learn it.

We all enjoy a leg up now and then. I too have screamed up and down the motorway, calling my voicemail whilst steering with my knees and far too busy driving to stop for fuel. Success can be very difficult, stressful and dangerous, trying to please everybody all the time. This book just aims to bring experiences, anecdotes, phrases and some well-tried and tested and shared methods together to offer you, the reader and learner, some help along the way. So if you are like I was, then slow down, pull over, take a break and make a little more time for... you!

By reading this book or anything similar, you are, if you weren't before, taking positive steps to at least try to help yourself to simply gain a better understanding. Reading every management book available will not guarantee you being the best manager, but it will certainly guarantee you have a better understanding of the subject. So, what's my biggest learning curve? Learn as much as you can. Learn it well and aim to become the very best in your field and enjoy its successes, however you measure it.

Finally, if you wish to be the best, study your craft. Management is just that, a craft or a skill like any other job. Look at anyone who is the best in their field and ask yourself how or why? Why is Sir Richard Branson so successful? He might not be the best manager, but he certainly must be one of the best of British entrepreneurs. He is simply good at building businesses. But only because he has studied the subject matter and developed it all his life. Jeremy Paxman is possibly one of the best political interviewers we have ever had. He has been a political journalist and reporter all his life. Sir Alan Sugar? Again he may not be the best manager to work for, but undeniably he has built and developed his empire all his working life. Bill Gates? And so on. They all come with lots of chance and risk-taking, but mainly with years of experience and practice, with good and bad decisions and lots of self-belief and determination, will power and stamina to simply succeed. They have all gone on to do just that. They succeeded, to become what they are now. Put simply, you don't just get good at something overnight.

When I was starting out as a young 'wannabe' there seemed to be a sea of books and authors on 'the big M' subject, all offering advice. I too began to read and every book I studied helped me understand just a little more. There was no overnight miracle and I didn't feel I had been liberated. It, like most things, was a 'work in progress'. And now, even though I have researched, studied and taught the subject, it still does not make me the best manager. It simply means I have a better understanding and am still learning.

For the purpose of our exercise, we may assume that we are developing into a new self or have identified a new opportunity to change and develop into a new direction. This could mean a promotion or a change of location, depot or branch or just returning from a training seminar or annual leave. Whatever we feel comfortable with, decide on a start date and plan out how we will go about practicing our new skills, working in order of self, staff, standards, stock and so on. If nothing else, this approach will just give you a psychological fresh start and, once you have a plan, stick to it, keeping the self and staff (the people factor) at the foremost of the plan. This approach will help give you an opportunity to start acquiring and building on what you have already, assisting in longer-term goals of gathering the best tools for your toolbox. The Seven Ss system is designed to be used constantly. Its purpose is as a sound management programme, creating a cyclic check across all disciplines and in cyclical order. Once comfortable with the system of the Seven Ss, including all seven disciplines in order, it can also be used to design and deliver structured presentations on longer-term planning strategies – monthly, biannual or annual planning, and even for five-year planning.

I very often had at least a one-hour commute, so would use the drive time for self, in the morning and at the end

of the day, analysing and reflecting on my own performance and any imminent topics. Then once at my workplace I would focus on staff, with team briefings, huddles,
one to ones or just quality time with my teams. Once the
people issues were settled I would walk my business and
focus on standards, looking for maintenance or development areas. This would include walking my managers
and/or teams around their respective areas of responsibility, coaching and developing along the way. This
approach allows for stock observations and strategising
and, therefore, sales planning for the day. This of course
will allow time for shrinkage and service activity as the
day goes by. Again each topic should be revisited over the
course of the day, threefold if needed, checking in on each
subject. This is not helicopter management. Quite the
contrary. The skill of observations and monitoring, supporting and coaching carries great weight with great outcomes. With this core structure at the heart of our work,
people will begin to notice we are serious, reliable, consistent and more confident about our role and that we
show a better understanding of our position and responsibilities. Only then can we start building a brand. As we
cycle through each topic we will become more aware of
our own actions and awareness. It will allow us to reflect
on how we behave and our time management skills will
develop. We will decide how much time is required for
each topic and, as we develop our business, weaker areas
will be enhanced and improved.

Although not absolute or guaranteed, each subject we
look at is a totally separate topic. To better understand
them they should be studied, researched and understood
separately, as they cannot possibly be covered in one

book. Being human makes us all very complex creatures and one rule will not suit us all. Also, we will see as we read that there is much more detailed text on self and staff; these, being the human elements, are clearly the two most important units.

"If you don't know where you are going...
then any road will get you there."

Lewis Carroll

"Failure is simply success in progress."

Albert Einstein

History

To know where you are going, it is important to know where you have been and sometimes a little history can be a help. Besides, it is always part of the learning programme to understand the history of something. To understand the events surrounding and leading up to World War II, you have to do some homework first to understand the history and events surrounding World War I. Knowing your history should help prevent making the same obvious mistakes again and, therefore, increase your chances of success.

After hunting and gathering gave way to farming, around 8500 BC and once farming was proven to be a better-managed way of feeding communities along with new productions of metal and mineral objects such as farming tools, the absolute need to trade (swap) these farmed and mined goods came about. Since no one farmer could grow everything, people chose what they would or could farm or mine, depending on their environments, and then trading (swapping goods) with each other became the norm. Humans had figured out how to trade very early on. It is suggested that since a circa of 3000 BC, humans were setting out on missions of water-bound trade, and by 1000 BC, with coins used as money, merchants were becoming senior and revered people of societies. But managers and management did not just grow out of trading. Pharaohs and ancient kings still needed people managers to run and govern their empires. Temples and pyramids had to be built and the scale of these projects required masses and masses of manpower. Armies too needed to be managed and again thousands of people needed to be fed, clothed, exercised, trained and, of course, beaten and whipped into line. This all required managing and these roles were not necessarily for profit. There were also growing ideas about how to treat people and how to get the best from the slave or customer from Babylonian to Tudor times. After coinage was introduced the simple art of trading was replaced by the act of bartering, which has now been around for centuries and still exists and thrives today.

Much like today's need for economic growth, merchants and sailors were trying to go farther and farther in order to find more rare, exotic, exciting and unique products with which to trade. The farther they went the more revered and famous they became. Ancient society marvelled at these new products and wanted more and more trading routes. No ancient society wanted more than the Romans, who were prepared to literally go to the 'end of the world' to find new products with which to trade. Eventually as villages grew into cities the butcher, the baker and the local candlestick maker had to meet the needs of the customer with 'customised' products as well as nascent marketing techniques.

Much later, mainly around Victorian times, the beginning of the industrial age brought vast new challenges of a customer base and the business proprietor would now likely never ever meet their customer in person thereafter. Today the Internet makes that problem even more extreme, but it also offers new opportunities to bridge the gap. After the First and Second World Wars life in commerce and, therefore, management, changed radically, both here and in the US. The absolute 'need' for services and manufacturing had changed. In peace time things are bought and sold for different reasons. The procurement of products was no longer a require-ment of 'the war effort'. Products were no longer shipped around and sold purely for need. Now there were other requirements: 'wants' and with wants came profits. Businesses were now unshackled from the old parameters of tight governmental budget constraints and sales, profits and margins could now be freely explored, developed and pushed in a bid to gain the upper hand to become dominant against rival contest-ants and to secure the futures of those businesses. Rival contestants were no longer military departments, but real live people wanting and demanding better lives and better ways to live. People were tired of suffering and making do. Western populations were tired of all work and no play. This was evident nowhere more so than in America and Britain, especially after the harsh condi-tions of the First World War, the thirties' Great Recession and, of course, the forties Second World War. Economies were on the move and companies and people were feeling liberated.

From the '20s onwards, economic prosperity experi-enced by many countries during the 1920s (especially the United States) was similar in nature to that experienced in the 1950s and 1990s. Each period of prosperity was the result of a paradigm shift in global affairs. These shifts in the 1920s, 1950s and 1990s occurred as the result of the conclusion of World War I, the Spanish flu, The Great (Wall Street Crash) Recession, World War II and finally the Cold War.

Liberated themselves, with a need to harness these new 'wants', companies from all sectors explored and experimented in many different ways to supply these new, fast-growing demands in a bid to promote and sell more. To do this they would need a different type of manager from the old stereotypical, bank manager types of the forties. Moving away from the '50s and now into the '60s, these armies of managers would have to understand their new customers and have to have a real hunger to grow their customer bases and deliver their market-driven results to new private shareholders. Managers would now be asked to be innovative, be outward thinking, creative, vibrant, enthusiastic and successful, but above all accountable. As more and more companies thrived, management and management style too was on the move. But mangers were not made. They were developed and then they evolved. Like the demands of their customers and growing companies, they too were now part of evolution revolution.

More than one hundred years ago people like Henry Ford were trying to improve the production of their staff to improve their production output, to, therefore, increase their sales and profits. Factory owners were timing processes with stopwatches to understand how to improve production. Since these times, successive waves of new thinking have refined our understanding of what management is and what managers do. Studies and experiments lead to the establishment of scientific management, which focused on workers' tasks and performance. With the explosion of the industrial age proprietors and factory owners and scientific theorists examined how individuals who supervised workers and work processes functioned. They examined these 'managers' planning, commanding, co-ordinating, organising and controlling the process of work and its production. These examinations and inquiries led to a better understanding of administration management.

In the '20s and '30s other studies were conducted to establish if improvements in environment enhanced production. The results were positive not only from the general workforce, but also from both the administration and production managers too. It emerged that even the very studies themselves had an impact on these mangers and their productivity as they too responded to the attention being paid to them as subjects in the study. From here on it became clear that an understanding of human behaviour would be a fundamental important component in the evolving knowledge of management.

The three main aspects to emerge from all these studies back then, in both industrial Britain and America, were: 1: Strategy in the behavioural underpinnings of production. 2: Support administration of production and work. 3: Science of production. (Already S words were becoming essential to highlight and underscore meanings). So then began the evolution of management. In the forties, after World War Two, theories were tested and developed at the Tavistock Institute of Human Relations in London, which drew on Maslow's theories and laws of hierarchy and of human needs and wants. These studies concluded the requirements of social, technical, environmental and emotional understandings within an overall organisation. After the post-war depressions, economies grew, so management needed to evolve to keep pace with booming economies. Production and sales had to improve, so more studies took place to determine if behavioural science had a place and could be employed in the management of an organisation to bring about positive and successful planned change. So then, way before I came along, we already had three Ss of a sort and, as mentioned, these areas focused on strategy in the behavioural underpinnings of production, which was research into the people aspects of work: self, staff and standards. This would investigate how work behaviour affected production, followed by studies into support administration of production and work, again an input focused on stock sales and shrinkage and finally the science of production, which focused on the final output. From now on theories of work, employment, relationships and practices would be heavily tested. After the science came the psychology to find a better understanding of the motivations of workers and managers alike. These activities and processes continued on through the sixties, seventies and eighties. These practices later evolved into what we know today as human resources management and, through these principles, working within a now established framework, managers would be guided. Here the three Ss are: 1: Strategy in the behavioural underpinnings of production. 2: Support administration of production and work. 3: Science of production.

"Those who do not know their history are doomed to repeat their mistakes."

George Santayana, novelist and philosopher

"If you can dream it, you can do it."

Walt Disney

"Your brand is what people say about you when you're not in the room."

Jeff Bezos, founder of Amazon

"Your brand is only as good as your reputation."

Richard Branson, founder of Virgin

Success

Success comes from the Latin word *Successus*. The accomplishment of an aim or a purpose. With a favourable outcome. A positive result. Better than hoped for. Whatever its history, we all know it when we see it and we always enjoy it and its rewards. It is built into our very DNA and does not need to be taught to us. The reason for this is that with success (a tangible state of fact) comes happiness (an emotional state of the mind). It is a feeling we get when the brain identifies the correct moment and releases chemicals into our body that then allow the transmission of electrical pulses through our nervous system. These chemicals are called endorphins. When released, endorphins react with receptors in our brain, which then reduces the perception of pain, suffering, sadness and misery and, therefore, give us a feeling of hope, gladness and general happiness. When we are happy we feel safe, more confident, more eager and more willing to experiment or take risks. It's not uncommon to hear people talk of a getting an endorphin rush. Sex, exercise, even red-hot chilli peppers have been accredited to these euphoric highs. Now, when you watch people's behaviour with each other it becomes clearer and easier to understand how some people just bounce off each other.

There is a strong desire within most of us to succeed and be successful with a need or want to feel that sense of achievement. Why? Well, I guess it's just because we are human and because we can. It is what sets us aside in the animal kingdom. Animals do things purely to survive, because they need to; however, we humans have learnt to do things because we want to. Because we have learnt that we can. It is how we have evolved. We have learnt that we can do things if we want and with that comes reward. Over time we learnt that if we do certain things we gain a satisfaction or emotional reward. From as early a time as 'hunter gatherers' we learnt that satisfaction or success makes us feel better inside and gives us an emotional kick, a sense of pride or a feeling of well-being or achievement. A good hunter who could provide regular food would be revered within his peer group and even promoted socially to chief of a tribe or head of a village. This was the emotional reward or what we now regard as success. As we work our way up, trying to be a great 'hunter' it can be easy to forget all the things that we learnt along the way and things that were passed on to us by our elders, some bad, but mostly good and very useful. We also learn how to deal with the bad things and the poor methods, or the terrible management practices or treatment we receive from others and not always in our working life. Sometimes we see and learn from how families and friends behave. As humans we all behave differently and can do and say terrible things that can have huge impacts on others and ourselves, so we learn that we can even learn to use the bad stuff too, to help us improve. That's what they call a win-win.

We humans like to be liked and we have learnt in more modern times that if we are successful at work then generally we are liked more by everyone a whole lot more. Not just by our bosses and paymasters, but by our friends and families too, and that makes us feel so much better knowing they are all so proud of us and delighted with us when we have earned that reward, bonus, promotion or pay rise, or even that new company car. However, on reflection, a note of caution as we must not confuse success with happiness. Happiness has been defined as a temporary heightened positive emotional state of the mind that has a profound positive effect on our person and personal lives. Success is a more permanent measurable and, therefore, tangible state of fact. Being successful is not always about climbing the corporate ladder for reward. Success can just simply be a basic level of happiness or just how relaxed, comfortable and in control of our lives and work we really are. Being successful is not always material and should not be measured so. We can also be successful and happy with what we have. We all have our own values and standards.

Born post-war and growing up in a northern shipyard town, my parents came from humble beginnings and my father from a council estate. As a child I remember both my parents working hard to bring up four children during the '60 and '70s. My father also worked away an awful lot, but we always lived in new-built modern semi-detached houses with gardens. We always had a car and many Butlin's holidays, with picnics and trips out to the Lake District or beach most weekends and, overall, a mostly happy upbringing. Now, we, all four children are successful in our own ways and my parents are retired. After more than 60 years of marriage and now in their golden years, they live together happily in their comfortable detached bungalow with neat manicured gardens, mortgage and debt free, without any of today's modern stresses. This is their success. This was their objective, so, I guess, job done! For me as a divorcee and unlucky with children I can only admire and applaud their amazing achievements in happiness and success. We can be rich in money, knowledge, love or just contented happiness. Success can be measured in many different ways and given different weightings. We are all different with many different wants and needs, but whatever our success and however we measure it, it will always have a positive knock-on effect in our personal lives and, therefore, have a long-lasting effect on our general well-being.

As humans, we need, want and enjoy success. Obviously, sex and red-hot chilli peppers are probably way up there at the very top of the scale and, as humans, we do not need to experience that level of success all of the time to function well on a daily basis, but clearly we still require to be stimulated on occasions to remind us that we do need to experience some success from time to time. It is also now medically known that the absolute opposite of all this energetic chemical rush is depression. Not enough and/or a continued lack of these experiences can lead to people to feeling very negative, down and depressed.

If we look at an average, hard-working person for a moment, who, over many years, has successfully built up their life and, through these successes along their way, are fairly happy with their lot. Then, through no fault of their own, they may be made redundant.

Quickly over a very short period of time this obviously leads to financial hardships, which triggers unhappiness and can then lead to domestic problems, which could then lead to housing and marriage and relationship problems. As serotonin and endorphin release mechanisms are closed down, eventually there are fewer chemicals being produced at all and fatality can even occur after this point, of what seems, no return. Even the very thought of this scenario evokes sadness. So now let's imagine a work colleague who was having a tough time at home, where serotonin and endorphins weren't being released and then they had to work in a drab, stifled workplace where there is also no stimulus to release these chemicals. No success and no chance of success. Sometimes a new boss or manager arriving or being promoted can help colleagues release a little of this excitement with a chance of success or a little hope. This is your best time to act.

"Success breeds success." That's what they say. When success chemicals flow it can make a whole world of difference. It can lift the spirits of any team or individual. It can make you want to get up early and go in to work before your start time. It can even change the mood of a nation. It may also even explain our behaviour when falling in love. New lovers are constantly praising each other, mentally and physically. Telling each other how beautiful the other is or how wonderful they are and constantly adoring and touching each other. One chemical reaction leads to another, causing a knock-on effect. Now it seems easier to understand why new, young lovers cannot seem to keep their hands off each other. These chemical reactions can last for days or weeks. Similarly, when we are told how impressed people are with our presentation we will want to do another one, bigger and better. When we are told how impressed the CEO was on their recent visit to your store, or your boss telephones you to congratulate you on your last sales figures or just quite simply being told you are loved, it inspires you to move to the next level, looking for the next fix. This is success.

After receiving a successful promotion or taking over from a predecessor, we could easily go into a new office or depot and immediately, 'on a wave of success' and with good intention, begin to tidy a warehouse, a stationary cupboard or a canteen or just have everyone help clear their desks and tidy up in order to reintroduce some improved standards. We would mobilise our teams and manage the project, enrolling and involving colleagues to assist us, and we would make it part of their day's work, demonstrating that we require a different standard in the workplace. The achievement would be instant, because these things are what I call 'fixed assets'. They are very black and white. Bins would be emptied in seconds. Desks would be cleared of junk in no time; floors can be swept and cleared in minutes. That warehouse or stock room might take a little longer, but the end result will be better than we started with. Is this a success? Certainly it is, if that was our objective. If we just want the office, desks or warehouse cleaned and tidied for just one day then mission accomplished. But normally this is not the main objective. We would usually prefer that the space be kept cleared all the time. We will have used our management skills to deploy our team into the clearing-up exercise. But the real success will come when those standards we set out with are maintained over several weeks or even months. True success will come when the people we involved maintain those set standards consistently all the time. It is when we transfer our management skills over to them so they can manage the situation for themselves. This is true success. Your team no longer needs you to help organise them into clearing the office. They think about it and can do it and want to do it for themselves now. They now have a healthy thought process habit of doing it for themselves. These are the 'non-fixed assets'. These 'non-fixed assets' are the paradigm shifts, the thought processes we encouraged and invoked, assisting the team to willingly take on tasks for themselves. It is the empowerment and ownership we inspired in them. This is the unseen work of management. We used our management skills to complete the task and set the standards. What remains now may be some slight, soft intervention periodically to remind them of the task. That is the management skill. So now we have the foundations of successful management.

Arguably this could now be seen as showing signs of leadership, but it is extremely important not to confuse the two. Many books have been written on both and leadership is definitely a different topic that we can only hope to touch on in this book. When success arrives it is perfectly healthy to recognise and embrace it. As humans, we enjoy the emotion of satisfaction and the prize of a 'well done' and that sense of achievement. It gratifies us with that warm feeling of accomplishment and releases those all-important endorphins that we talked about. However, like any addictive drug, it is important that we manage our intake of success and, of course, endorphins. Although we won't overdose, we will need plenty more happy moods in the days and weeks to come so managing success is just as important as receiving it and looking for it. Pacing oneself and looking for small, but frequent rewards is a good practice, as is with teams and colleagues. Drip feeding success is more important than just winning one battle. Pacing oneself is vital for team morale and as team leader or manager you may well be the one who can release that success bit by bit.

Serotonin

As well as endorphins, our bodies also rely on a substance called serotonin. This is another neurotransmitter that works in conjunction with endorphins. Serotonin is often referred to as the happy chemical. This makes it an important substance for well-being and mental health. Although studies are inconclusive, it is thought that a lack of serotonin results in depression. Apparently at this date it is not clear whether depression causes a low level of serotonin or vice versa. It is also thought that it has a role in diet, hunger, anxiety, phobias, bone health, sleep and sex. With sleep it is believed to assist in regulating our body clock cycles. Again studies are ongoing, but it is also believed to be found in the human gut and stomach lining. This all helps to give us a sense of satisfaction and well-being.

Sacrifice

Success is not free and does not come easily, unless you are that fortunate, miraculous, micro minority percentage to stumble on something magical. For the rest, success, however we measure it, will come at a price. Even if you do stumble on something magnificent it will still normally take great effort to make it into a success. The idea is the easy part, as is aspiring to climb the management ladder for example. Getting that idea to market or getting that promotion is where the sacrifices and struggles begin. Whatever we feel success is, we must be careful to put a measure on it and then when we have considered all options and weighed up the pros and cons we must be prepared to sacrifice whatever it takes to make it a success. For some it will simply be a burning passion. For others it may be they see a goal or ambition and for others it may just be to make a fast buck. Whatever the driving force, the success we crave will take sacrifice. Elon Tusk, head of Tesla cars, is reported to have worked 100 hours per week for 15 years. Richard Branson is reported to have mortgaged himself to the eyeballs initially. Alan Sugar says he missed out on his education. I myself hardly saw anything of my young daughter as she grew up and my wife (back then) clocked me at 75 hours per week. My father worked away a lot contracting for better wages and missed out on his kids growing up. Many people have cashed in policies to finance their dreams, suffered divorce and lost friendships in their bid for success. So be wise and take care; success will demand sacrifice, struggle and usually some suffering.

Speculate to Accumulate

As with sacrifice and success, this old business phrase is well used and most people understand it more once they have tried or used the theory successfully. It normally refers to finance or investment in a business, but it can also refer to time, deeds and acts or thoughts and ideas. The meaning is you will only get out what you put in and sometimes the only way to forge ahead with a project or idea is to push so hard that you give out more than you are actually likely to get back in the early days. In the early years of setting up my own company I ran the business at very little profit, simply to beat the competition and just make a living and pay the staff wages. Profit was a luxury that would come later. Only when I had firmly established the business did I feel comfortable to improve my profit margins. I speculated that I could get to x, y or z. Once I achieved this I had accumulated enough industry knowledge, skill, staff, orders and equipment to deliver a greater product. Each BBC *Dragons Den* programme shows how the inventors have speculated to get their ideas and inventions off the ground and they further speculate that the Dragons will invest in their ideas to help them accumulate market share, profits and longer-term wealth. In return, the Dragons speculate their investment in that invention being worthwhile in order to share in the project's prosperity. It is worth remembering, however, speculating is a balanced thought process based on facts, in the hope of a gain. Many managers will speculate to accumulate based on their industry knowledge and experience to achieve favourable outcomes.

Seek Forgiveness, not Permission

Whilst we speculate and sacrifice ourselves in our quest for success another skill that should be carefully used, and I hasten to add after years of political management experience, is the rule of 'better to seek forgiveness than to beg for permission'. This approach to tackling problems is usually attributed to highly independent, proactive, experienced and knowledgeable managers. Here they act out or instruct on a process with decisive actions, but calculate the success or outcome as worthy of the cause. Knowing they should probably seek their line manager's or company's approval before proceeding, they prefer to move forward, feeling they have complete autonomy or they believe the success of the project far outweighs the risks and to deliver a high level of success with little company or peer input is worth the risk. Here they speculate on the outcome being so successful that it will impress and please the company. The risk of getting it wrong is purposely minimised and the chance of a 'pleasant' surprise to bosses demonstrates their skill and knowledge as independent, but safe managers or leaders. If the success is not forthcoming, they can always seek forgiveness, as their objectives were wholly admirable and with good intent. This approach to work normally requires an open and liberal free-thinking environment where negotiations and discussions abound. In today's increasingly competitive world of IT, companies that can encourage (or afford) this style of management are firms like Google, Apple and Microsoft where mistakes (input) can be undone (financed), but the successes (output) can be huge.

"There is absolutely no substitute for success. Failure is the fog through which we glimpse success."

Anon

"Success is on the far side of failure."

TJ Watson, founder of IBM

Management

They say the definition of management is the process of dealing with or controlling things or people. To accomplish objectives through the application of available resources. The act or a manner of managing, handling, directing or controlling. This is a much-debated topic with each author trying to stamp their own mark and opinions from their perspective. Don't rush too quickly to look up the definition unless you have a strong will to live! Don't run it through a search engine; you'll be up all night working your way through all the suggestions. They can be mind-blowing and some of the definitions are almost nonsensical, jargon driven, elaborated, glossed up, fluffed out, technical paraphrases and just mumbo jumbo. "Management is the process of reaching organizational goals by working with and through people and other organizational resources" (management innovations wordpress.com) or "it consists of the interlocking functions of creating corporate policy and organizing, planning, controlling, and directing an organization's resources in order to achieve the objectives of that policy".(businessdictionary.com). Another suggests "the act or skill of controlling and making decisions about a business, department, sports team, etc." (learners dictionary.com) or "a function that coordinates the efforts of people to accomplish goals and objectives by using available resources efficiently and effectively."(petrowiki.

org). "The way something is handled, careful treatment, supervising skills, or those in charge of a business or group." (yourdictionary.com). Wow! And so it goes on and on. I guess they're all correct if you break them down, but I prefer to stick to what we know on this one. *The Cambridge Dictionary* suggests it is 'the control and organisation of something'. *The Oxford Dictionary* states it is 'a process of dealing with or controlling things or people'. I absolutely agree with these two English versions.

For me it's just about getting things done, efficiently and quietly. If we stick to the dictionary definition as already mentioned then we are surely on the right path. It does not matter whether you work alone or are part of a team, a husband, wife or parent. If you are a teacher, supervisor, team leader, department manager, or even if you employ one person and even if you are a teenager with your first motorcar, you will at some stage of a normal day 'manage'. We are human. It's one of the things that we do best. We manage. As people, we cope and get by, to live another day. We constantly battle the forces that are put in front of us and we manage. Even a young teenage girl with her first car will probably subconsciously manage her father by attention, love, negotiation and attrition to keep her vehicle roadworthy and on the move. Taken seriously in the commercial professional sense, I say management is the art of motivation with the heart of innovation.

So the question now becomes what sort of manager? In this book, we are aiming our sights as a commercial or business manager at some level, but whether we are a team leader, branch manager or area manager, the point to remember is we already have management skills gathered and collected along the way from previous roles. What becomes important is to understand what skills we now have and how best to harness them. Exploring who, what and where we are, we can really begin to focus on where we want to be and accomplishing what we set out to do. Understanding these differences has been my journey of learning over the years. Studying and practicing the skills I have found, pinched, borrowed or been given over the years has helped me realise that I wish I had known all that back then!

We have said do not confuse management with leadership. To reiterate, these are absolutely two very different subjects and again people have written many books and theories on both subjects. Leadership, like management, is a huge topic that can take years to understand and master and is far too lengthy for just one book. Management versus leadership has been debated for years. We can explore leadership a little later and how it constantly crosses paths with management, but for now have a look at this quick example: a manager will source you and get you the best ladder for the job, but a leader will show you which wall to lean it against! My example is 'a manager will provide the brollies or the parasols, but a leader will provide the weather forecast'!

Though not absolute, 'the Seven Ss' and 'all the Ss' serve as a sound reminder of note for reference. It is not suggested that they be better than other models, but does offer a logical method to create some semblance of order to help us understand that we can always stop, reflect and look at the Ss to assist in regrouping, taking stock and starting again to reach the successes we set out to attain. 'All the Ss' can apply to any management role in any sector, whether in agriculture, energy, finance, manufacturing, production, public sector, supply, retail or tourism. I believe the same rules apply to all management areas.

A note worthy of mention, especially at branch or area level, is that we are still very much the foot soldier or the sergeants. We are still one of the troops and we must never fall into the trap of just dishing out the instructions. A good manager will always convey procedure, policy, politics, party and priorities without fear or favour in a passionate, dignified, balanced and professional way. Being so close to our staff, it can be easy to explain everything as 'because they said so' or 'I've been told to tell you'. This style of management is only the 'stick' or fear only method without a carrot and frowned on as a real cop out, showing poor management and leadership. Our teams will constantly ask what, why and where, so we should develop our sales and lobbying skills and, therefore, ourselves, into a better leader.

Read, read and read, then learn. To be great is not to be good and we should use our free time wisely. Two hours on an Xbox might relax us, but it won't enhance our management skills or career. My advice is to pick up a book in any form and read. Read, study and learn. Then review all we have learnt to date and then experiment and practice it. Practice really does make perfect. Teach yourself by doing things and trying out. Make written or mental notes to see how you are faring. Remember all the good and the bad. Even working for a bad manager will teach us something. Ask oneself which manager was the better to work for? The one who constantly telephoned us on their days off or who constantly pops in whilst on holiday, or the one who leaves us to get on with it in their absence? Which one is really in control? The manager constantly popping in is demonstrating control, but what type of control? Is it positive to not let your team get on with things?

In the first two subjects we will focus on self and staff. These two are clearly the most important topics, as they concern us, people. They are also important because they are the only two Ss that are so variable and non-fixed. We, being humans, are such complex creatures and learning to deal with people can become a lifetime's work with thousands of books being written. Factories, offices, products and services are all fixed assets but people are variable assets and can make or break a business. Do not underestimate these people variables. We, like our team, are variable assets and all should be looked after carefully. Get it wrong and it can spell disaster for you. Get it right and success can surely be yours.

Styles of Management

So what style of manager are we or are we going to be? There are several styles of managing, from autocratic or democratic, laissez-faire to transactional or transformational. When considering career success, tangible qualities often come to mind, such as the type of work and salary. But one critical factor to our success is leadership style, both in how we manage people and how we like to be managed. Effective managers can improve productivity and employee morale and reduce turnover. There are six widely agreed-upon management styles commonly used in today's business world, but I have highlighted three more. Each of these styles has their own strengths and weaknesses, and a person can use more than one style, depending on the situation. It should be noted that often managers do not set out to be one or the other. They usually gravitate to their natural alignment based on character, training and opinions. Only once recognising various styles do we wish to improve and adapt.

Autocratic

Autocratic managers make decisions unilaterally, without much (or any) input of subordinates. This unilateral format can be perceived as a good management technique if the right decisions are made, and it can lead to faster decision-making, because only one person's preferences need to be considered. However, this style of management can drive away employees who are looking for more ownership of decisions and more autonomy. In times of crisis where time is limited, use of autocratic management is permissible, but extended periods could lead to high turnover.

Consultative

This form allows for more discussion than an autocratic method, but is essentially dictatorial. As the name suggests, a leader in this form consults his or her employees, but ultimately the leader makes the final decision. Decisions attempt to take the best interests of the employees into account, but also focus on the business. This type of management style often leads to loyalty from employees included in the decision-making processes, but those who are left out are more likely to move on. It can also lead to a dependency of the employees on the leader.

Persuasive

Also similar to autocratic management styles, a persuasive leader maintains the final decision-making control. However, he or she makes choices based on the persuasion of subordinates. Employees will convince their manager of the benefits of a decision and the manager will make the final decision. This is a great option for managers who need input from experts, but still keeps the final decision-making up to them. This does not work when employees do not support management and choose not to provide input or do not trust decisions that have been made.

Democratic

As its name suggests, democratic managers offer employees an opportunity to engage in decision-making. This means all decisions are agreed on by the majority. The communications go from the manager down to employees and from the employees up to the managers. This style works when complex decisions must be made that have a variety of outcomes. However, democracy does slow down decision-making and could be inefficient at times.

Laissez-faire

This style is the complete opposite of autocracy; employees are allowed to make the majority of decisions, with management providing guidance when needed. The manager in this case is considered a mentor rather than a leader. This style of management is popular in start-ups and technology companies, where risk-taking is encouraged. However, it can lead to difficulties in making decisions.

Management by Walking Around (MBWA)

This classic technique involves management by listening. Managers gather information by listening to the thoughts of employees who can stop problems at their source. When using this type of management style, managers must be counsellors and not directors. A good decision will be well received and respected by all. When employees do not support management there can be problems in MBWA management.

Transformational

Transformational leadership inspires people to achieve unexpected or remarkable results. It gives workers autonomy over specific jobs, as well as the authority to make decisions once they have been trained. Some of the basic characteristics of transformational leadership are inspirational, in that the leader can inspire workers to find better ways of achieving a goal; mobilisation, because leadership can mobilise people into groups that can get work done; and morale, in that transformational leaders raise the well-being and motivation level of a group through excellent rapport. They are also good at conflict resolution. All of these traits make transformational leadership a good fit for many types of business. Transformational leaders are sometimes call quiet leaders. They are the ones who lead by example. Their style tends to use rapport, inspiration or empathy to engage followers. They are known to possess courage, confidence and the willingness to make sacrifices for the greater good. They possess a single-minded need to streamline or change things that no longer work. The transformational leader motivates workers and understands how to form them into integral units that work well with others. There are marked differences between transactional leadership and transformational leadership. Transformational leaders specialise in working to change the system, solving challenges by finding experiences that show that old patterns do not fit or work, wanting to know what has to change, and maximising their teams' capability and capacity.

Transactional

A transactional leader is someone who values order and structure. They are likely to command military operations, manage large corporations or lead international projects that require rules and regulations to complete objectives on time or move people and supplies in an organised way. Transactional leaders are not a good fit for places where creativity and innovative ideas are valued. This style is most often compared to transformational leadership. Transactional leadership depends on self-motivated people who work well in a structured, directed environment. By contrast, transformational leadership seeks to motivate and inspire workers, choosing to influence rather than direct others.

These leaders work within the system and start solving challenges by fitting experiences to a known pattern. They will want to know the step-by-step approach and minimise variation of the organisation. Another way to put it: transactional is a 'telling' style while transformational is a 'selling' style. The term 'transformational leadership' was coined by sociologist James V Downton in 1973. Leadership expert James Burns defined transformational leaders as those who seek to change existing thoughts, techniques and goals for better results and the greater good. Burns also described transformational leaders as those who focus on the essential needs of the followers. Many current leadership theorists agree that principals of transactional and transformational leadership can be combined for ideal outcomes for both management and the workforce.

Asian Paternalistic

An Asian paternalistic style means that the manager makes decisions from a solid understanding of what is desired and best by both consumers and staff. Managers must appear confident, with all answers, and promote growth with harmony, often even if hiding harmful or sad news is required. Like consultative and easily confused with autocratic and dictatorial; however, decisions take into account the best interests of the employees as well as the business, often more so than interests of the individual manager. Communication is downward. Feedback and questioning authority are absent, as respect to superiors and group harmony are central characteristics within the culture. This style demands loyalty from the employees, often more than to society's rules in general. Staff turnover is discouraged and rare. Worker motivation is the status quo with East Asians often having the world's highest numbers of hours worked per week, due to a sense of family duty with the manager being the father and staff being obedient children, all striving for harmony and other related Confucian characteristics. Most aspects of work are done with a highly collectivist orientation. It shares disadvantages with an autocratic style, such as employees becoming dependent on the leader, and related issues with seniority based systems.

System Management

System management should not be confused with styles of management. These are very different from each other. Management styles are how we manage. Management types are what we manage. There are two system management phases. These are object and process/project management, both requiring different approaches. We can manage things in many ways, but really only one of two in the main.

In the first instance we manage for objects, where we maintain something as it should be or as it was intended, a product or an object such as a car for example. We do not enhance or develop the product, but we simply manage our involvement and activity with that car to maintain it exactly how the manufacturer intended it.

We use it for the purpose intended and we replace the parts like for like or exactly when required. We wash and polish it to prevent decay and we valet the interior in the hope of minimising its depreciation. Classic cars can receive intense object management. Similarly, it may not be our job as a manager to develop a building we work in or the furniture within that building. That would be the role of a head office property and/or refurbishment department. As a middle or branch manager, for example, our role would be simply to invite window cleaners, plumbers and air con engineers to keep the building maintained to the company's required standard in order to operate or fulfil rental contracts. This would be our involvement on a weekly, monthly or yearly basis. This is object management, pure maintenance. Other examples of object management could be the enforcing of company rules and guidelines, tax laws or health and safety regulations, policy or best practices. As managers our job is not to agree or disagree with them, but to act on them and ensure we sell these practices or systems positively to our teams, monitoring, measuring and maintaining their existence mainly for compliance. With this type of object management there can only be one standard. Other examples of this can be items clearly priced with a company sales ticket or not, or the product demonstrably works to the standard intended or it doesn't. There is no real leadership here really, just good old-fashioned maintenance management.

The second type of management phase allows us to manage in order to improve and develop something, a type of management that allows us to enhance something perhaps less tangible, such as a team of people or a stocktaking or refund system. Here we can move, make and mature and we are allowed to show creativity, flair, vision and leadership. Here we can take an issue, a person, a product and move it on, reshape it, develop what we have and make it better than it ever was and grow it. This is process management. If we stay with the car metaphor a little longer we can use it again to explain the process management system. We could find a beaten-up, old scrap car and, using the process management system, rebuild and develop the car back to its former glory and back to how the manufacturer originally intended it to be. Now we are on a management journey to develop and improve on what we have. With process management we would use the monitor and measure theory to allow us to see the end vision or goal. The standard or measure is what the car would have looked like when it rolled off the production line 60 years ago. Measure assists us in getting to the 'maintain' or object phase. Once accomplished, when we are satisfied with the measurement (show standard) we can, for now, finish with process management. Once satisfied with 'what a good job looks like' we can switch across to object management once more. As discussed, this is where the washing, waxing and polishing come into play. Of course, as any sensible manager knows, resources can be rare, exhausting or expensive to continue with the process phase and you may make a management decision to call a temporary halt to the process (development) phase for a time. You may have only managed to get the car up to a basic, but roadworthy state. At least you can drive it for a while until you are ready to move back to another phase of process management at a later date. In the meantime it would be wise to opt back for object management (the maintenance). It would be reckless and careless to allow all our hard work to be undone.

What if we completed the car rebuild project? After a short period of object management (maintenance) we could choose to go further and this time push the manufacturer's '60s standards for today's modern driving. We could return to process management by exchanging the old drum brakes for improved discs, exchange steel wheels for lighter alloys and introduce power-assisted steering, upgrade shockers and fit wider, newer radial tyres. As a commercial manager we could do this with sales, profit margins, stock or indeed people. But remembering to get to the move, make and mature stages of process we first need to pass through the monitor, measure and maintain stages of object.

We can see that we can use these two systems of management in tandem or separately in an order of our choosing to obtain our goal. We can switch from process to object (development to maintenance) and then move back to process as we push for higher or greater success or standards. It is important to note that, once we understand the concept of object and process management, there is the danger to drop back from object to process. If we can keep with the car analogy just a little longer, please take this into consideration. After spending hundreds of hours and possibly thousands of pounds on the process management phase (development) and if the rules of object management (the maintenance of the achieved standards) are not adhered to, we could easily find ourselves slipping back to day one, having to engage back in process management and having to rebuild. In summary, once you have invested all your time, patience, learning and money and developed a good team, look after it. Engage deeply in object management. Wash, polish and wax it until it shines brightly.

However, the examples show that once we have taken over a new role as manager it will be necessary to initially engage in the art of object management and ensure things are how they were intended. Taking over from a predecessor will often mean this approach is needed from the outset to check and ensure that all is well and in place. Once we are satisfied all standards have been reintroduced, we can implement the process system, allowing things to be developed. This is where we as managers can shine with leadership and success. This process phase is where we can achieve best results. It could be said that object management is just good basic management and process management is where great leadership, vision and skill starts. This is where real career success lies.

Superiors and Subordinates

This area of management can be described as a process whereby the superior and subordinates (self and staff), knowing their positions in the process, jointly identify and agree on common goals. Both then define each individual's major areas of responsibility in terms of inputs and results expected, then they agree measures and guides for operating as a unit and assessing the contribution of each of its members toward those goals. In layman's terms, the manager, being the superior, guides the team, the subordinates, into identifying and realising what needs to be done and then agreeing on a system of operation by empowerment and delegation to achieve the outcome. In return, the team or staff, agreeing to be subordinate, will work to support this outcome. Whilst most people understand this arrangement, explaining the split rule or fifty-fifty rule will help in identifying and clarifying this superior and subordinate system. Even at management level this system needs to be present in order to promote clear working practices.

"Success is buried in the garden of failure."

Rick Wakeman, Keyboardist, writer and producer

"Managers provide parasols and umbrellas.
Leaders provide weather forecasts!"

Chapter 1
Self

As we have said the subjects we look at in this book are totally separate subjects and, to better understand them, they should be studied, researched and understood separately and cannot possibly be covered in one book. As a positive starting point here we discuss and look at how important this self subject really is and how it interconnects with all the other Ss. This subject is crucial to the survival of, well, everything. The only reason we have commerce, finance, manufacturing, building and retail is all because of us, people. It is so important not only that we realise how each subject connects with the other, but in order to start somewhere, and in the best possible management style, it would be prudent to start with our most valuable asset and resource: ourselves.

'Self' looks at who and what we really are and what we are about. Firstly, our management starts with us and no one else. Secondly, nothing is truer than action speaks louder than words. We are and will be measured and appraised on what we do, not what we say. Whether it be the forces, families, politics and our private life or in leisure activities, we are all judged on what we actually really achieve in life. To this end we must deliver on what we say, which leads us to building our brand.

Self, out of all the Ss, must be the hardest subject to tackle, since sorting ourselves out always seems harder than sorting out others. We always seem to have plenty of good advice for others, but when we try to sort ourselves out it can seem to be quite a struggle at times as we do not like criticism, we do not like advice and we often know best and do not want to listen. I would suggest that we, the reader, the learner, always use the first S as an anchor or hook in our memory to help us remember how we feel, reflect and like to be treated.

Self rhymes with health and wealth. I am a great believer that, if your brain is fit and healthy and your thought processing can remain positive, your body can remain healthy too and we can keep the endorphins flowing. They say one thing leads to another and research shows how happy people live longer. Happy people seem to do better in life and suffer less or appear to deal with fewer traumas and go on to better things. I believe my parents succeeded through happiness and their wealth is how they pleasantly and quietly enjoy their stress-free retirement in comfortable surroundings. Happy, settled couples prosper longer together with a strong will to look after each other regardless. This strong sense of love, belonging and need for each other conditions the body to release a steady flow of endorphins, keeping the body and brain fitter and healthier for longer. Sadly, it is proven that when we lose a long, long loved partner, we, too, start to fail. We often say they 'died of a broken heart' and it is easy to see why when people have been together for a lifetime and then lose someone. All that positivity and energy is gone and the endorphins cease to flow. Using positive energy, athletes prosper on and off the track, privately and career wise; with their years of dedication and positive mental attitude (PMA) they seem to deal with life, happy with their inner self and, because of their regular, albeit heightened, level of exercise, their bodies constantly release the right flow of chemicals. So here the message is think positive, encourage yourself to take ownership, take charge, stay fit and exercise well. Even mental medical advice is always to encourage plenty of physical exercise, whether it is a game of squash or a regular walk. Never be the victim, as your positive mental attitude will make you feel better about yourself and your future successes. In other words, do not rely on others for good weather. Carry the sunshine with you and then share it.

Have you ever been too busy driving to stop for fuel? I'm sure most of us have at some time in our careers or lives. I believe we are all guilty of it, quite literally too. It is one of the easiest crimes to commit. I certainly have, both metaphorically and also quite literally. The act of doing it is not really a crime, but preventing it happening over and over possibly is. The lesson I learnt from this tough practical experience was to literally take time out of a busy day's schedule, stop, start and do some serious time management and also to stop at a filling station or carry some extra fuel! Believe me the long walk down a dark, busy highway in the rainy winter, dressed in only a thin suit with an empty jerry can, is not remotely humorous. It is what they call 'busy fools'. Scurrying about with good plans and good intentions, but struggling to get where we would like to be or achieving our goals. This example is both a metaphor and a true life practice. Try excusing yourself for being late to a 'time management' forum because you ran out of petrol! Also the walk on a dark, wet and windy highway can easily be a metaphor too for just bad management. This could symbolise poor decision-making and wrong choices, going off the rails or just losing sight of the true path.

The fuel part can also be used as a metaphor for food, drink, sleep, leisure, rest and, of course, endorphins. Are we fit and healthy? Our mind and our body are all we have and without these two things, mobile phones, diaries, computers and company cars are useless to us. Do we fuel up our car regularly and do we put our mobile on charge at night, but ignore our own body? Are we fit and healthy? Do we look after ourselves or do we constantly run on 'ines'? Nicotine, saccharine or caffeine? Do we have a balanced diet? Could we do more exercise? Could we spend more time with our family, loved ones and friends? Are we in a happy place emotionally and financially? Do we cope with life in general? There are a lot of questions being asked of us. If we answer yes, then excellent and well done, give ourselves a pat on the back and then try to understand why we are where we are. In a good place. If we found some of the answers a bit of a struggle, then that is excellent also; give ourselves a pat on the back, as we have acknowledged an area and already begun the process of being proactive with a will to improve ourselves in a positive manner. Now we can begin to work on fixing self and items we feel are perhaps not in such good shape.

Being proactive is intervening and changing the outcome. It means an act of response during or prior to an event, thereby changing the outcome prior and not after. If we can be fit and healthy, which naturally helps release good chemicals to the brain and helps with a positive outlook, we can be brave and confident enough to see things in other ways. I used to tell myself as long as I am honest and true, whatever bad people do to me over my lifetime they will not have a lasting effect on my long-term path or course. We do not have to be a slave to cause and effect. The alarm clock rings (the cause), making you wake up (the effect). By being positive, you can change the cause in advance by changing the alarm time or cancelling it altogether. This is our PMA, our positive mental attitude. Athletes and successful people carry it with them, like their own good weather.

We all have an image of a stereotypical manager. A smart, sharp-cut suit, Filofax, briefcase and a mobile phone used for absolutely everything, a company car, an umbrella and so on. These iconic images suggest they are always ready and prepared, positively and confidently, for anything. Why do we need to carry a diary? What's in the briefcase? Why do we constantly use our mobile? These items support and give these people confidence. Put simply, the reality is that these items are tools of the trade. A manger is a tradesman or woman and, like any good tradesperson, will keep his or her toolbox close at hand. The suggestion is, using our tools helps us remain positive and proactive and continue having a positive mental attitude. This is the very first tool we should place in our toolbox. It is no good being a comedian if we do not feel happy and funny or we have nothing funny in our toolbox. How can we succeed if we have no happy disposition and no jokes? Ironically, this itself is no joke!

Self-esteem

In psychology, this phrase is used to describe a person's overall sense of self-worth or personal value or just exactly how much we appreciate and like ourselves. Self-esteem is seen as a personality trait that helps us as individuals feel that we belong somewhere and gives us a steady feeling of confidence that we are part of something bigger than just ourselves. It allows us to feel part of a social group or gathering and with skills, interests and knowledge that are valuable to a wider group or social class. High self-esteem is extremely important if we are to feel successful and is a sensory reward of prowess we all experience when things are moving positively for us. We can improve our self-esteem through circumstances and/or others can improve it for us by offering genuine praise and admiration. Serotonin and endorphins will flow and we can enjoy the status and admiration. It is also known as our ego. I liken it to us all having our very own ego bucket. The natural point is probably midway when our bucket is half full (not half empty). When we are on a high with self-esteem our bucket is completely or almost full and, vice versa, when our bucket is empty or very low we will show many signs of sadness, depression, misery and self-pity and so on. To understand success we also need to understand that our ego buckets can be emptied by ourselves and/or others quite easily if we do not look after our buckets. Events and/or people can have a habit of drilling tiny holes into our buckets, allowing our ego to slowly drip or dribble away and thus emptying our bucket. Looking after our bucket is a way of maintaining successful deeds and actions or remaining relevant in the groups we circulate in or how we look for new ways to please and inspire others. This will maintain our self-esteem and keep us feeling good and worthy. Our ego can be like a piggy bank and saving money. It can be a long, long slog to build up and maintain a reasonable amount, but so easy to spend it.

Self-determinism

Self-determinism is not genetic determinism. Our past should not determine our future and there is no reason that it should. We should not play the victim. We should be brave and look inward first to see what and who we are. We are what we are. Should we be what our parents were? Do we think that because our parents were x, y or z we should be too? Some believe in the theory of genetic determinism. This implies that, because our parents behaved in such a way, our lives would automatically mirror theirs. Many believe in this theory of genetic determinism and allow their lives to naturally mirror that of their parents or older siblings. As the sayings go, 'he is just like his father', 'she is her mother's daughter', 'like father like son' and 'it's in his genes' and so on and so on. Does this really have to be the case? I would challenge this theory and say we are what we are and if we have the great foresight to see what we are and make a conscious decision to change, then we take charge of our lives and become our own masters and, therefore, decide our own fate. If we are to accept genetic determinism as de facto then we merely surrender ourselves to fate (cause and effect) and allow circumstances to take over our whole purpose in life. This does not mean our parents are automatically defunct and not worthy of opinion or the examples set by them do not count. For those of us lucky enough to grow up in our parents' presence we should, of course, remember their teachings and examples they set. We should cherish the knowledge and wisdom they gave us, but we do not have to accept their shortfalls or poor behaviour. The shortfalls of their generation become our generation's opportunities using process management, each generation improving on the previous, sometimes two steps forward and one back, but overall there should be slow and steady development. What held them back then should not apply to now and, in our highly civilised European liberal world of today with equality, diversity and education opportunities, the time has never been better for us to grow, develop, push ourselves or reinvent ourselves. Neither should we believe that because his father was a bum he too should grow up into a bum. It is true there are many occasions where this happens, but this is not genetic determinism. This is just plain uneducated mirroring of behaviour and accepting the examples we have grown familiar with and statements like 'it is all we have ever known' or 'that's how we have always done it' or 'I voted Labour because my dad did' simply cement that underdeveloped behaviour for the future. We can change at any given time of our choosing, but, like smoking or dieting, only when we feel naturally ready and willing to accept the change needed. Sometimes that change will come about from absolute necessity; other times it will come from a real urge of enthusiasm and because we really want to. However it comes, we should, like the managers we used to work for, remember all good examples they gave us and improve on the poorer ones. By doing so, we will overcome genetic determinism and project our own personal self-determinism.

Some Serious Thinking

This book does not aim to cover all the many wonderful topics that relate to management and neither do we have the time, but I do feel it worth touching on these two. They are sequential and simultaneous thinking. Decades of research has shown our brains are divided into two compartmental halves. Psychologists have known about these two halves for many years and it helps them to understand us when we suffer from mental health issues or for more serious inexplicable issues such as autism, Asperger's or dementia. Once explored it can be most interesting whether we are left- or right-handed! Once understood, it is also interesting to note that left-handed people can become most frustrated with life at times, as their whole brain wishes to use the full extent of their simultaneous, Van Gogh-thinking (right-thinking) brain part, but, being a minority, living in a majority of sequential, left-sided brain part, right-handed, rule-of-law world, they are forced to conform (contain and cage the chimp) to sequential thinking. Therefore, they suffer from the stifling of ideas, creations and dreams and can also find themselves in bother with rules and regulations of society.

Sequential Thinking

The left side is for everyday life and daily tasks, this being the world most of us (the majority) live in. This is the predominant left side of the brain and, if you are right-handed, you will tend to use the left-hand side of your brain more on a regular basis. Take a look at how many left-handed people there are compared to right-handed people. The left side of the brain deals with sequentials. These are the specifics of our everyday life and even the sequential functions of the left side of our brain fall under the rule of 'all the Ss'. Statistics, specifics, solutions, solving, systems, standards, safety, security, survival, sensibility and self-esteem. Though not exhaustive, also sensibility, speech, sound, sight, smell and statistics. Numbers, time, orders, instructions, commands, management, conclusions and outcomes, reason and purpose. This is what they call the sequential thinking brain part. Here the brain uses all the aforementioned and collates whatever it can to analyse or break down and split apart in order to sort and reorganise and finally prioritise in an analytical orderly fashion.

Simultaneous Thinking

The right side of the brain, however, constantly wants to drop into free fall. This is the simultaneous thinking side. This is the impulsive, picture and image side where logic and time has no relevance. Here there is no real order and the orderly S rule cannot apply. Here there are no outcomes, but is where the dreams, inspiration, wants, creativity, chaos, innovation and imagination come from. This is the side that left-handed people tend to use the most. The Van Gogh side as I call it. This is the side that refuses to listen to reason and just wants to project the first thought that appears. A number, a colour, a word or a sentence or an image. Here sparks fly and wonderful things can appear and can be where all our creative flair and inspiration comes from.

To help us understand others and to compound this brain thinking issue further, now may be an appropriate time to introduce Professor Steve Peters' *The Chimp Paradox*. Peters offers us another view on how the mind likes to work, learn and tackle issues, such as dealing with situations, learning, instructions, requests, emotions or stress. In Professor Steven Peters' book, *The Chimp Paradox*, he refers to these two parts of the brain as the chimp and the human. In his book Professor Peters explains, but also supports other theories and tests of how the brain generally likes to work in two halves. One half of the brain is operated by the human (the owner) and the other half operated by a chimp who has to be kept in a cage. It should be obvious which one he calls the chimp. Here one part of the brain often outwits and out manages the other half, giving us sometimes quite crazy, hare-brained ideas or seemingly irrational answers to rather simple situations. The chimp can even escape his cage and cause all sorts of other mischief. For example, when people panic under stress it is often that the human part of the brain has allowed the crazy chimp half to reply to the situation. The chimp is a very emotional being. I mention this as it is of much significance and importance that we reflect, first to understand ourselves and how we think and learn, and then of course that of our people and teams.

Once we know and understand this we can then begin to be better managers. Ask ourselves are we a simultaneous or sequential thinker? If we are a simultaneous thinker (left-handed – minority) trying to manage a sequential thinking (right-handed – majority) team, then we may experience frustration when we suddenly realise why we are the only one coming up with all the ideas! Similarly, if we are a sequential thinker attempting to manage or develop an unruly (chimp) simultaneous thinker, take a moment to reflect on how our approach may be skewed.

An interesting fact to help embed this point in your psych and support this theory of serious thinking and it may be of interest to know that simultaneous thinkers (left-handers) include Bill Gates, Van Gogh, Charles Darwin, Leonardo da Vinci, Isaac Newton, Rembrandt, Benjamin Franklin, Michelangelo, Einstein, Picasso and, of course, Abraham Maslow... oh and me too!

Self-critical Analysis (SCA)

It can also be useful to try some self-critical analysis at times. To help we can remind ourselves every day of the Michael Jackson song, *Man in the Mirror*. The lyrics read 'I'm starting with the man in the mirror'. This is the perfect place to start to become a more positive person. I always carry my own weather with me and, therefore (for my benefit if not for others), wherever I go there is always sunshine! Being self-critical is a great way to explore a little and gauge where we are. Ask ourselves: are we highly social or are we seen as too busy for others? Are we short-fused or do we analyse a lot? Do we jump in first or reflect? It can be a good practice to keep copies of any old personal appraisals or work reports. Collate them chronologically and look for patterns. Look for both positive and negative. Do a gap analysis of where we feel we should be and ask: can we improve where the gaps are? All this is much easier said than done, of course, but if we can accept development areas then we will begin to have a better understanding of who we are and where we need and/or want to be.

Sanguine

We could try to be more sanguine and adopt a glass half full, rather than half empty, approach and learn to be more proactive rather reactive. A positive outlook always helps to enthuse others. Being ever the optimist means there is always another way. My parents used to tell me 'can't means won't try'. If you say you can't it normally means that you haven't tried hard enough. Or 'where there's a will, there's a way'. Again, if the will is great enough we always find a way to get or do something. Being human, generally, if we want something badly enough we usually go and get it. This is the proactive optimism we all carry. Even when faced with the fatality of a firing squad, the ever-optimistic officer commented to his men, "Don't worry, chaps; they're using old rifles, which tend to jamb!" I would not suggest we obscure our vision from everything else, as it is important to remain real and balanced, but positive vibes really do rub off on people and do have an impact on teams and individuals, as we all know. From football teams to rescue teams, to charity aid workers to office staff, from partners to friends or to our children. If we are proactive we will drive ourselves and our teams forward to successful outcomes.

We could ask ourselves are we happy, are we comfortable and content in our role? I have been lucky only to feel sheer dread at work only once in my career when I was going in to work. After six months, the drive to work got worse and worse and I dreaded the prospect of another day in that place, so I forced myself to call in sick. I later resigned and moved on undented, but with lots of learning curves. It is absolutely critical that you feel comfortable in the role, for you will have confidence, again creating positivity. Never be afraid to ask for help. It is absolutely not your job to know everything. That is why we have specialist staff, teams and specific recruitment campaigns. Remember the people in your team are generally the best at what they do, so we should never be afraid of asking them to show us how. I have never known a team colleague not willing to show me how or why they do something. If you have a bad boss, ask someone else. We will look at this method of learning in the staff section a little later, as it is another great tool for our toolbox.

Another trick is to learn how you like to learn. Most of us learn visually and like to see how something is done. Ask yourself which school subjects did you like the most, which teachers and why? Take a look at the Honey and Mumford model. Are you an activist or a theorist? Who and what are we? A reflector or a pragmatist? Analyse yourself and try to begin to understand who you are and where you are presently. This is a great way to start the change in yourself. Understanding how we like to learn will help us understand how our team members might like to learn. This is known as a paradigm shift, where you begin to see things from a different angle. From another person's perspective. This will speed up your teaching and training time with yourself and others.

There's another very true old saying, 'put your own house in order first', and I always add 'before we look over the garden fence', which suggests that we take charge of ourselves and our abilities before we start to interfere in organising someone else. Or, 'people who live in glass houses should not throw stones'. Don't criticise others if you don't want criticism. After much research with his students Professor Jordan Peterson was quoted as saying about younger inexperienced people, "If you can't make your damned bed quit waving placards at corporations." And we 'risk inflating our own egos by dealing with the problems of the world'. One of my earliest lessons as a young manager, dabbling in leadership, was to be, or rather, try to be, whiter than white and as free of criticism as possible. This is certainly most difficult and needs constant attention, to act and set the example, but not to be a hypocrite or say one thing and then do another. This is one of the first steps to leadership and a vital skill, because we constantly cross from management into leadership and good management requires great leadership.

Stop, Start!

This exercise in remaining positive is vital to developing ourselves. Learning to stop and take stock, as they say, is possibly the best way for us to understand the past, the present and the future. Where are we now? Where have we been and where are we going and where would we like to be? This is our gap analysis. I am a big believer in understanding our history before moving forward. For example, understanding why the culture of a business is what it is before we start changing or trying to influence it makes a whole lot of sense and can become part of our strategy. However, once we get 'on a roll' it is not always easy to stop, especially when we are driven by positive vehicles such as ambition, drive, enthusiasm and a desire to succeed. Many things can prevent us from stopping for that all-important fuel. Time or lack of it (we think) is a massive factor. Also, peer pressure can be problematic, forcing us always to look busy or task orientated along with many other commitments, constantly holding us back. This is why 'stop, start' (time management) plays such an important role. Good planning and searching for strategies can be so important. So learn to stop and take stock. Learn that it is okay to sit at a desk 'apparently' not doing very much. From team leader or supervisor to junior manager to director, thinking is what we are paid to do, thinking about the best way forward or looking and searching for a positive change in events or outcomes. Planning and strategising are all part of being a manager. If under pressure, simply explain to people 'I'm thinking'! 'Stop, start' is probably one of the most import tools you can have. Leaders and managers need time to think. Positive ideas do not always gush from a tap in the brain. They often need stimulating and encouraging, unlike rash, negative and stupid ideas that do seem to flow so easily from that chimp half of the brain. So, very often we need to stop, turn off the tap and then, only when we are ready, slowly turn it back on again, but only when the human half is ready and in control. Ask yourself, how many 'stop, starts' do you have in a day or week? It will be less than you think.

Start with the End in Mind

In his famous book, Dr Stephen R Covey suggests that one of his best habits was 'start with the end in mind'. This is an excellent way to help us understand how we should prioritise. He poses the question: what would we want written on our headstone and what would we like the speakers (friends and family) to say about us at our funeral? If we wish people to speak highly of us, we should start as we mean to go on and begin making a difference now. I call this branding. How we are remembered in death will be from our deeds and actions from this day on. These results become our brand and this is how we will be remembered. The results of our actions stamp our brand onto our good name. This requires great foresight and planning, but again with thought we can plan an outcome that is acceptable and satisfactory. Once we begin to plan something we begin to achieve it. As Walt Disney once said, "If you can dream it you can do it." If we really do want that job, plan the end result. Plan how we intend to get there. This will only lead to positive outcomes. At the very least we should learn to carry some extra fuel in the trunk of our car. Believe me, as I said, it beats walking miles down a dark and wet highway. Moving on through the ranks of management I realised there were now many different ways of learning and a lot less painful than walking down long, dark roads.

The Power of Branding

Google, Lego, Duplo, Pot Noodle, Tampon, Learjet, Sky TV, Durex Tupperware and Pyrex. *We don't vacuum; we Hoover. We don't web search; we Google, and we call four-by-fours Jeeps. We don't use social media; we Twitter. We don't message; we text. We use a Stanley knife rather than a safety blade and we don't drink Cola, but instead Coke. This is the power of branding!*

"As we focus on the use of the Seven Ss one will see that we are building a brand. Not a company brand, but a personal brand. People buy from people and, using the Seven Ss, we can build ourselves up into a brand that people will recognise and become emotionally attached to. If we are consistent in the use of the Seven Ss people will take notice of this consistency and will, over time, come to trust us through our behaviour. This will not happen overnight. (The Hoover Company took more than 50 years to establish itself as the world's leading vacuum manufacturer of its time.) Consumers do not emotionally connect with a product. Instead they connect emotionally to the brand. Therefore, build a brand around the product. Make yourself the brand and not the product." Once we learn how to develop our management style, we should begin with a structured plan and, using the Seven Ss, what was once a product (manager) potentially develops into a brand (leader).

Sparsity of Effects

This principle is also known as the 80-20 rule or the Pareto principle named after Vilfredo Pareto, an Italian engineer and philosopher. He noticed that people in society seemed to divide naturally into what he called the *'vital few'* or the top 20% in terms of money and influence, and the *'trivial many'* or the bottom 80%. Later he discovered that virtually all economic activity was subject to this principle, in that 80% of the wealth of Italy during that time was controlled by 20% of the population. He noticed that 80% of Italy's wealth came from approximately 20% of its population. This was supported by the fact that 80% of all the land in Italy was owned by only 20% of the population. He then found that this rule applied to many other things in life and it was certainly true of human efforts and endeavours.

In our application it is used in both time and effort and put simply means 80% of our invested input is responsible for 20% of the results obtained. Put another way, 80% of consequences stem from 20% of the causes. Put simply, you will never get 100% output from your 100% input. Once we have an understanding of this rule it is easier to see how we should use our time wisely and develop ways to work smarter and only by 'stop, start' will we see this in its true light.

We often see others who appear to be busy all day scurrying and pedalling about, but they seem to accomplish very little. This could possibly be because they are busy fussing and working on tasks that are of low value and consequence, the 80%, but procrastinating on the one or two really important activities, the 20%, that could make a real difference to their companies and to their careers. The truth is that the most valuable and rewarding tasks you can do each day are often the hardest, but have the better payoff and rewards and the success of completing them can be tremendous. Before we begin work we should always ask ourselves: "*Is this task in the top 20% of my activities or in the bottom 80%?*" The rule for this is to resist the temptation to clear up the small things first, the 80-percenter stuff. The 80-percenter is generally the easy stuff that you could probably delegate to others. If we decide to start our day working on the 80% low-value tasks, we will always develop a habit of continually starting and working on low-value tasks.

If we have a list of 10 items to accomplish, two of those items will turn out to be worth more than the other eight items put together. A sad fact is that most people procrastinate on the top 10% or 20% of things that are the most valuable and important, the '*vital few*', but busy themselves instead with the least important 80%, the '*trivial many*' that contribute very little to their success, because they are desperate for some success and the human nature in us is that we will readily take some form of success even though it is not exceptionally stretching. We naturally accept the successes from doing the easier stuff, but with little reward, and fall into the trap of not stretching ourselves or reaching for the higher goals. As a manager, it is now evident that, in order to reach a worthier success rate with greater rewards, it pays to be selective in what we choose to do. It pays to think about the 20% stuff that will give us much greater success. Now we can see that, in fact, 'less is more' and it is far cleverer to work 'smarter and not harder'.

Sharpen the Saw

We have looked a little at how our brains work and what makes us tick. We have learnt how we learn and how others like to learn. So finally, now we have taken a good long hard look at ourselves and know that taking time out to analyse is all positive stuff. We may now agree that slowing down and using the tools we already have (our brains and senses) can help us achieve personal goals and targets and make us better persons. We can now begin to make better decisions with longer-term plans for ourselves and, therefore, our staff and teams.

Steven Covey tells a great story about a struggling lumberjack, toiling and sweating in the midday heat to chop down a quota of trees for his logging boss before sun set. Looking physically stressed, facially vexed and sweating profusely under the pressure of the task, a passing walker asked the woodcutter, "Whatever is the matter?" The woodcutter explained his dilemma and emphasised how difficult a task it was to fulfil the lumber quota. The walker noticed the lumberjack's unopened packed lunch, water bottle and unused saw sharpening kit. The walker suggested the lumberjack stop, replenish some energy from his lunch and water, sharpen his saw blade and continue his task after the peak of the midday sun, refreshed and with a freshly sharpened saw. The wood cutter looked at the walker in disbelief and replied. "Stop! Rest? Are you crazy? Don't you realise I have to fell all these trees by sunset?" Clearly he was feeling extremely pressurised to fell all the trees his boss had marked out before nightfall. He was sawing and sawing and so conscious of the pressure and time restrictions he never once dared to stop to sharpen his saw or change his blade for a newer one. He finished the job, but he went home late with a bad back, blistered, swollen hands, hungry and thirsty, with pulled muscles! Also the age-old saying that 'procrastination is the biggest thief of time' is certainly true. Do we sit on a problem for an excessive amount of time? Do we bury our head in the sand and put things off? Learning to work smarter, not harder allows us to introduce the Pareto rule, better known as the 80-20 rule.

Smart Appearance

Whilst we look at smart we can pause quickly to look at our appearance. If we present ourselves smart, we present us, the brand, as a clean, crisp and organised individual well-groomed and well turned out. We should always have clean and ironed shirts and trousers with polished and well-kept shoes. Choosing what to wear from day to day is also a skill that shows that we do not only have two shirts and we are the professionals we wish to be. We do not wear cheap plastic belts with statement buckles with skulls and crossbones or footwear so fashionable they become a talking point or outrageous shirts or skirts that are more suited to a nightclub. Investing some money into your clothing and wardrobe is vital to making a very large and simple statement and how you should look whilst at work is a wise investment. Clean hands and manicured fingernails with properly washed and groomed hair and a clean-shaven face complete the appearance. Although tattoos, piercings and unshaven is fashionable these days it still gives out a poor and lazy message that we wish to be the same as all the fashionable in-crowd staff on the team rather than stand out alone as leaders. These appearances can still invoke the wrong message and, therefore, a different brand. By taking the time to shave and dress properly we are laying down foundations and setting the standards for our subordinates and colleagues alike. This is what a great brand looks like.

Styles of Learning

Before we close off this chapter it may be worth taking a closer look at the Honey and Mumford model. As with sequential and spontaneous thinking it is first important that we understand how our own brain ticks and secondly how the brains of others tick. As we have decided to improve our management skills (the fact that we are reading this book right now could suggest that we are), it would be a good practice when managing others, especially when we manage others by telling, teaching and showing, to identify firstly how we personally like to learn and secondly how our people and teams like to learn. Having a basic understanding of these learning styles and principles is obviously very wise, but also allows us to be more adept and empathetic when dealing with our people. This in turn not only humanises us by respecting the needs of others, but wins respect and speeds up learning times and, therefore, gives us quicker turnaround on results.

To help us with our self-critical analysis and working smarter, not harder, we can ask ourselves how we like to learn stuff. How did we like to learn back in school? None of us are born with common sense; we simply have to learn it. Like everything, common sense has to be taught. A child will not know that a boiling kettle can scald until told or shown. This is why we have chemistry and science labs in schools, but we so often, very easily quip to others 'to show some common sense'. We can ask ourselves how we like to learn. They say we all remember our best teachers, possibly because they got the very best out of us and helped us develop the most, but how? If we are to better ourselves and then others, then improve everything around us, we need to be better equipped. Knowing how we learn and enjoy our learning only accelerates the process.

On the back of previous learning, teaching and manage-ment research mainly by an American philosopher David Kolb, in 1982 two English colleagues, Peter Honey, a chartered psychologist, and Alan Mumford, a management development advisor, published a paper on learning styles. Through their studies they proposed there are four main learning styles and as humans we develop natural or habitual patterns of acquiring and processing information in learning situations. It became proven that we all prefer to learn in slightly different styles and that style leads on to how we like to manage. These four styles of learning are assumed to be acquired preferences that are adaptable, at will or through chan-ged circumstances rather than being fixed personality characteristics. The traits of these four learning styles are developed over time and we learn to move through stages, possibly cycling through all four. Initially, probably from a survival instinct, to help us learn and move on quickly we tend to adopt only one style. Later as we mature and develop we may retain the same learning style, but adopt and experiment with the styles in our management approach, cycling through and trying out all four until we feel comfortable in the application of each. Finally as we mellow and mature with our experiences we adapt and opt to use all four, becoming a little of everything.

Based on the foundations of David Kolb's *Experiential Cycle of Learning* publications, Peter Honey and Alan Mumford devised a way to allow people to find out how they themselves liked to learn and what learning styles they have developed over the years, such as activist, pragmatist and so on. Once their papers were published this allowed managers to explain and find out how their teams like to work. With the Honey and Mumford learning styles, we too can become smarter at getting a better fit between learning opportunities and the way we learn best. This makes our learning easier, more effective and more enjoyable. It saves us tackling our learning on a hit-and-miss basis. Equipped with information about our learning preferences, we'll have many more hits and fewer misses and, therefore, more successes.

After completing years of work on how people prefer to learn, Honey and Mumford concluded that one of them was the pragmatist and activist, whilst the other was a reflector and theorist. Ironically, after applying their newly found formulas to their own learning behaviour, they discovered that one supported the other in the duo team. One encouraged the other to take risks, the other encouraged his colleague to be more cautious, thereby creating a powerful relationship and proving the point that the whole equals more than the sum of its parts! Synergy! This would also help to explain how personal relationships work in domesticity. This is quite possibly why a relationship holds together with our partners. They say that 'opposites attract'. I would actively encourage you to try out your own tests and learning styles with a partner, close friend or relative.

Activist

These are those people who learn by doing. Activists need to get their hands dirty, to dive in with both feet first. They often have an open-minded approach to learning, involving themselves fully and without bias in new experiences. They are usually very confident people who are able to expose themselves to risk and learn by their mistakes.

Reflector

People who are reflectors learn by observing and thinking about what happened. They may avoid leaping in and prefer to watch from the sidelines. They prefer to stand back and view experiences from a number of different perspectives, collecting data and taking the time to work towards an appropriate conclusion. They are often quieter types of people who avert risk and formulate plans based on their reflection.

Theorist

These learners like to understand the theory behind the actions. They need models, concepts and facts in order to engage in the learning process. They prefer to analyse and synthesise, drawing new information into a systematic and logical 'theory'.

Pragmatist

These people need to be able to see how to put the learning into practice in the real world. Abstract concepts and games are of limited use unless they can see a way to put the ideas into action in their lives. They are experimenters, trying out new ideas, theories and techniques to see if they work.

Earlier we touched on how we like to learn and who our favourite teachers were and the teachers we remember affectionately all those years ago. But my question here is why we have fonder memories of some teachers and not others? How come we did well in some lessons and not others? Perhaps we enjoyed or did well in the subjects with the teachers we have fonder memories of? I propose the reason for this is that those teachers were just doing their job and being professional teachers. They used their management skills and found our learning styles in order to get the very best out of us. They managed us.

Whilst not set in stone and as we mature, we will see that we can adopt or swap styles as we change. From activist to pragmatist from reflector to analyst. This is how we naturally mature and grow, shifting slowly to eventually having a little of all four learning styles to help us get the best from our own learning.

Setting Priorities

Learning to prioritise does not come naturally to us all. Trying to work smarter and not harder can be easier said than done. Trying to implement the 80-20 rule constantly can also be difficult. Sometimes prioritising our day can take up half our morning before we even start. What one sees as important can be of little consequence to another or just not quite as important as last time. To help us see the wood from the trees it is always a good practice to stop, start and analyse things, to study a little, then see clearer before we prioritise. But if we don't stop to analyse we will never see the whole picture and, therefore, will miss out on prioritising correctly.

Understanding what is priority and what is not takes time and skill. Previous experience can tell us that we may not have made the best decisions in the past and now is our chance to rectify that by listing everything we see as a priority. Often things seem like important stuff, but really we learn that it can wait. Using the urgent and important rule will always help to clear the clutter and help us realise the smartest way to work. We know what is important and we know what is urgent, but often we mix the two together or get them in reverse, so here it is important that we take a little time to look at them both. They are not the same. Our daily work routine is important, but it is not urgent and, therefore, as we said, done daily and we will do it again tomorrow. Urgent things need to be done right there and now. Try drawing a priority matrix diagram like the one illustrated. Sketch the drawing to make the top left box priority number one. What would you put in this box? A number one box would be urgent first and also important. Top right would be quadrant two and in this space we would list items that we feel are not urgent, but are still important. The bottom left quadrant, number three, would be urgent, but not important and finally bottom right quadrant, number four, would obviously be not urgent and not important.

To understand the gravity of the rules, let us first look at quadrant four that we have just drawn. In here we should be looking to list examples like junk mail or cold callers, and trivial and meaningless chatter from colleagues. Anything that does not add value to your game. In fact, any item worth listing in this quadrant is not worthy of your time since it is neither important nor urgent. Anything listed in this quadrant will sap your energy and waste your time.

On the other end of the spectrum we have quadrant one, full of important and urgent things to do. Here we need to beaver away to achieve successful outcomes. Usually there will be deadlines and timescales. Possibly a disciplinary interview or a report for your boss. Where do we think a request for a report or vacuuming the office and emptying the bins would fit? What about feeding the company cat? Which quadrant does spilling coffee all over your keyboard fit into? You will have to decide since you will know your business best and what

Urgency

The Priority Matrix

resources you have, but I would always recommend we try prioritising in this way every day.

Senses

It may not be on our radar when researching management that we look at senses and initially it may seem a little odd, but our five senses are what allow us to learn and give us our perceptions of the world around us. From the moment we are born they allow us to start to understand our environment and surroundings. We use at least one of our five senses every second of the day and they are even on duty when we are asleep. It may seem very obvious, but often we forget to use what we were given at birth. Sight, sound, smell, somatosensation (touch) and fifth, instead of taste and for our purpose, we will use speech. We all automatically use these senses as and when without much thought. Unaware, we let them do their thing and feed back to us whatever comes our way, blissfully innocent of their potential.

In fact, when learning in the UK today, the VARK (visual, auditory, reading/writing and kinaesthetic) communication model is used significantly and acknowledges that all five of our senses are engaged when communicating with others, irrespective of the chosen method of communication. Engaging in small talk with colleagues, clients, suppliers and potential contacts, for example, is an effective means of breaking down barriers and establishing common ground. However, this superficial level of communication can fail to develop the all-important rapport and trust necessary for building strong long-lasting relationships. The visual, auditory and kinaesthetic theory demonstrates how effective communication is not just about what we say, but more importantly it's about the way we say it. The choice of words used to express ourselves communicates to others how we view the world. This in turn can influence how we are perceived and whether it is likely that trust and rapport will develop between the aforementioned parties. The VARK approach to communication helps us to identify our own communication style and to find others who share or complement our style and view of the world.

Sight and Sound

We can always look for a paradigm shift to help us see things from another point of view. I remember collecting my daughter from school once and thinking how casual and scruffy one young male teacher was, dressed in old baggy joggers and dirty trainers, compared to all the other smartly suited teachers herding the kids through the school exits. Visually he did not impress me at all. I later learnt he was the new and very successful PE teacher and just back from an overwhelming national netball victory win with the sixth formers! Here I learnt to open my eyes wider and look for the full story. Another visual skill is talking directly to people eyes wide open. Here we can learn to show empathy and interest with open, attentive eyes. Looking around and avoiding eye contact will not develop trust or even begin to show interest in your team.

When we consciously assess the potential of a relationship, listening is equally as important as talking. Listening carefully can effectively inform us whether rapport is in evidence from the outset and, therefore, whether the connection we are making has the potential to become long-lasting. So what if we really tried to use them skilfully, to better ourselves and improve our management and leadership skills? With a little patience and practice, we can all do this. We could use our eyes and ears more, constructively paying attention to greater detail. We could practice not listening to reply, but listening to understand. We often listen in order to prepare something to say in reply or retaliation. Instead, we should learn to listen to fully understand. Here we automatically begin thinking of what to say back when the other person is still talking, so instead of listening we are preoccupied with preparing a quick fire reply and, therefore, ironically not listening. If you have ever watched a politician being interviewed on TV, you will see that they repeat the question. This is what they call thinking time. We should first understand, then be understood. So with some practice it is possible that we can immediately, overnight with a little patience begin to start understanding others more with these few simple steps. How we use smell and somatosensation (touch) or kinaesthetic as managers is how we get involved and lead the way. The use of these senses are how we roll up our sleeves and get stuck in, hands-on and show our people that we are one, capable of doing the task ourselves and two, prepared to work alongside our troops to support them when *they* really think they need us. This is where we *sniff* out the situation and feel what our staff feel or think they feel. Here we can show that we too can feel the sweat and pressure of a role, task or job they are involved with. Finally after full use of the first four mentioned senses, only then can we use speech, to explain, tell, coach, or encourage our team into development. This is the rational, calculated and poignant way to communicate and coach our teams.

Speech

Often it is not what we say, but how we say it that make or breaks a conversation and, as already mentioned, when replying to others one should take time and literally pause for thought. This will demonstrate that we have listened, pondered and are consciously taking a thoughtful stance with thinking time. When addressing staff and colleagues it can also very be helpful to make a conscious effort to try to talk properly. Lazy speech and slang does not command respect, especially if we are looking for that all-important promotion. A healthy and strong command of the Queen's English can win so much respect. We can practice how we speak at any time. The drive to work is often a good time. Using our senses and deploying our skills in listening can very often resolve conflicts or problems and remove barriers from difficult or awkward situations. Once we have listened we should be speaking to our people softly and kindly in such a way that it will encourage and *allow* our teams to feel they can speak freely and express themselves better and more clearly. Speaking carefully and thoughtfully will inevitably result in a more positive outcome with more win-win situations. As Churchill once famously said, "More jaw, jaw less war, war."

Safeguarding

There is absolutely no one better or more qualified or responsible for the safeguarding of one's career than oneself and to help us do this I firmly believe that managers should have their very own personal plan. Succession planning was designed to fill gaps in a firms' labour market. If it works for them, I feel there should be as much emphasis given to this for individuals. This should not be confused with PCD (personal career development) or CPD (continuing professional development). PCD and CPD deal with what skills we have to date and where we are up to professionally and maintaining a required level of knowledge. Self-succession planning is about our future rather than the present and I firmly believe should be used in tandem, alongside our personal development. Self-succession planning is about planning for our future and setting out a road map to help us get there. As a company would use this process to protect itself from a future skill shortage, we too should use it as a goal-setting, job-securing strategy that will identify skills and training required to protect oneself from environmental work changes and identify a career path for us to follow.

Self-successive Planning

Do we have a self-succession plan for ourselves? This is a 'stop, start' moment. Stop and take time to reflect where we are, where we have come from and now where we would like to go. Do we have a five-year plan? Do we need a five-year plan? Have we achieved all we require? If we still have ambition and a will to develop, the answer will always be that we need a newer revised self-succession plan, a one-, two-, three- or even five-year plan of where we would like to be and what is needed to get there. Do we need more qualifications or just more experience? Do we need to finance our future development and if so how will we do that? Are there special courses needed to get us to a certain level? Could our current employer provide us with the required resources and training, or are there other firms offering better apprenticeships or internships? As I said earlier, I had one company sponsor my degree work. This is part of our succession planning. We will see how important this process is for our teams when we look at the staff section. If it is important for them, it must surely be equally important for us. We are all quite keen to update our CVs, but when we renew our CV we should also renew our succession plan and write it down, 'Word' document it and save it to our PCs or smart phones or write it up in a Filofax or notebook and use it for monthly reference. We can check in with ourselves anytime to see if we are on track. Although not fixed or set in stone and like any business plan, things in life can often change, but at least we have a plan and it will act as a guide. If we are not happy with our succession plan, stop and start again, but be reasonable, keep it real and keep our objectives and goals achievable.

Safety Spheres

Safety spheres are our 'comfort zones'. This term refers to a psychological state in which things feel familiar to us and where we are at ease and in control of our environment. Most importantly it is where we experience low levels of anxiety and stress and, in this sphere, uncertainty, scarcity and vulnerability are minimised, allowing a steady level of performance. Safety spheres or comfort zones describe how, as humans, we prefer our environments to be and given the choice we will naturally choose the safest. This is true of both our personal and business lives. As humans we all still have, genetically built into our DNA, the fight or flight stress response reaction system that allows us to operate in these various spheres.

I use safety spheres in two ways. The first way is the traditionally accepted approach. Imagine three large circles surrounding us or on a flip chart as in an archer's target. We are in the bull's eye. This innermost ring is our safety sphere. In this sphere, we are at our safest. Here we want for nothing and have all we need. We are comfortable without fear, stress or anxiety. Here, for example, in the bull's eye, stands the mother and, as a baby, we will never crawl beyond that circle (out of the mother's sight). This is our safety sphere or comfort zone. Stepping out of this safety sphere into the next, like a baby crawling into another room, initially raises anxiety and generates a stress response. This results in an enhanced level of concentration and focus.

Within the next sphere lies the optimal performance zone. The stretch zone. In this sphere, we can overstep our first sphere, crossing the line to see what else is out there and if we can cope. Like the baby in the next room, we constantly look back checking to see if the mother is still there. If things go wrong, we can quickly and easily move back into our first safety sphere where the mother (or line manager, mentor or friends and colleagues) are standing waiting to hold support and, therefore, offer us comfort until our next attempt. The third sphere is initially the danger zone or panic zone. This is a place where we have never been before and here we are at our most vulnerable and exposed. Here we suffer stress and anxiety, afraid of the unknown. However, as we move back and forth between these spheres our confidence grows and we find the first sphere of safety increases, pushing out and forcing the second sphere away into new territory and, therefore, pushing away the danger or panic zone as we experience and learn to understand the spheres' contents. Slowly over time as we develop and understand more, the danger zone becomes a comfort zone and, like an old tree, the rings grow outward more and more. Eventually the baby leaves home!

Venturing out into the optimal performance zone (where performance can be enhanced by some amount of stress) is good, as anxiety improves performance until a certain optimum level of arousal has been reached. Beyond that point, performance deteriorates as higher levels of anxiety are attained. As we have seen, beyond the optimum performance sphere lies the 'danger or panic zone' where initially performance declines rapidly under the influence of greater anxiety. However, stress in general can have an adverse effect on decision-making: fewer alternatives are tried out and more familiar strategies are used, even if they are not that helpful anymore. Optimal performance management requires maximising time in the optimum performance sphere, but requires consolidation time in the comfort zones too.

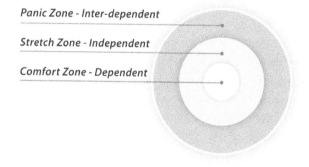

Panic Zone - Inter-dependent

Stretch Zone - Independent

Comfort Zone - Dependent

Safety Spheres and Comfort Zones

The second way of using the spheres of safety is by way of measuring our skill, knowledge and confidence in the form of dependency. As we mentioned early on in the book, very young people are, of course, dependent on parents or guardians or as new starters with a job or going to a new school we know very little and rely on a boss or a work mentor. Again we initially occupy the inner sphere and rarely venture out into other areas. As we mature and develop we feel we know it all and do not require any help, making us independent. Finally, as we mature further on in life we have all the skill and experience and knowledge gained from when we were both dependent and independent, but we now also realise we do not know everything and as professional managers we understand that we have staff to help and advise and we are not afraid to ask for help. We now enjoy a heightened level of dependency and this is known as interdependent. We know how and when to switch from dependent to independent. We can swing between the two. We know when to ask for help and advice and we know when we can autonomously act based on experience and knowledge. It is not possible to be interdependent without first developing through the first and second stage of dependency. Now we are interdependent and can operate freely and comfortably between all three spheres.

Swing the Pendulum

This is a skill and tool I found invaluable during my management years and I learnt to use it daily. This is a training method that is still a well-used favourite of the UK's driving instructing industry. I swear by this method of coaching and development, but suggest that it is very under used. Swinging the pendulum is a method used in conjunction with safety spheres during learning. The pendulum (the skill and knowledge level) is a support method we can use when training and developing others.

It is an instruction tool that we can introduce or remove from level to level in a learning arc, from left to right as a clock pendulum does. As people learn they move through knowledge levels until we no longer need to be taught or trained on that given subject. Anyone can learn to do anything if we put our minds to it and, once we commit to learning a new skill, we swing through phases and degrees of skill levels and confidence. The system recognises three levels of learning: guide, prompt and independent.

Learning is quite simply a habit. To learn a new skill our brain relies on the process of building a habit. This habit building process is an ancient survival skill linked to success or reward, but must first be triggered. For the habit to form effectively the brain will acknowledge three stages: the cue or trigger, the response and the reward. Our ancestors used this habit system as a primary reward to remember the location of food or water. Nowadays we use it for secondary reward to get us things we want such as a driving licence or a new job. A trigger or cue can only happen if the brain acknowledges a reward as an outcome. This is the reason to accept the behaviour in the first instance. This is the want. After the cue comes the response. This is when the brain computes 'if I do this that happens'; 'when I push this, a lid opens'. After the response comes the reward. The reward is the outcome of the action or thought. The reward completes the habit cycle and the action is learnt. As the action is learnt the brain finds quicker and easier ways to carry out the task, so the task becomes easier and more effortless, so much so that we can do the task without thinking. A simple example of this process is when a young child is asked to put some kitchen waste in the pedal bin for the first time. The child wishes to help and have a go. This is the cue or the trigger (the want). The child then learns by watching others or being told or shown that, if he or she steps on the pedal, the lid will flip up. This is the response. After the response comes the reward. When the lid flips up it allows the child access to dispose of the rubbish. This is the reward. As times passes the habit is repeated so often that the task is eventually carried out subconsciously whilst doing other tasks and thinking and talking of many other things.

Before a habit can be triggered, as a manger or tutor, we need to explain to the learner the habit process in full, usually emphasising the reward. We would also explain the benefits of using the pedal bin in a certain way, as this reinforces the cue or trigger and gives a firm reason to want to attempt the task. We would talk through and reiterate how and why the pedal bin works as it does. For more complex tasks we may use diagrams and charts, depending on how the learner learns.

We begin the teaching process by guiding. Once the habit is triggered we will only understand the basic first level of learning, which is being told or shown. This is guided. This is a basic level of cognitive understanding and does not bear much fruit until we have researched, listened to others, studied it or had a go for ourselves. Here further knowledge, practice, analysis and research is still required before we move to the next level. At the guide level, we would normally ask to be shown a task again or to have several attempts at doing something.

Guiding is telling and showing. This is the first stage of the brain forming the habit. We tell and show the child the pedal and how to stand. We explain how much force is needed and we demonstrate how to stand back to allow the lid to open. Being such a simple task, the child would only need a few attempts to achieve the reward and complete the task; therefore, our guiding need not last for long. In a more complicated task such as learning to drive, we will need to spend more time guiding on one action. To enable the response we would guide the learner several times to begin the habit formation.

As we practice the task or memorise the information, the brain builds bridges between its neurons and the sparks begin to fly. Since a habit is totally autonomous and can only be a habit when this event occurs independently free of other inputs, we need to step away from guiding. As the newly learnt action becomes easier, as a tutor we do not need to guide, so we can move to prompt.

The prompt is to encourage the habit to continue developing, but on its own. Prompting is a way of measuring how much learning has been retained and if the information and action has been recorded accurately. As humans we tend to forget things and we do not remember everything at first glance. We need practice, but what if we continually enter a password on our grandmother's IPad for her? Will she remember it? If we constantly grab the laptop from her and click on everything she should have for her, will she learn how, why and where to go for her next Google search when we are not around? The answer to both is clearly no. So after guiding, showing and telling we now take a back seat a little and establish how good the learner is at doing the task. Does Grandma understand now how the finger pad works? Does she remember what the Google icon looks like? Has she remembered where to click? If she does, we praise her of course. The praise tells her brain that it is doing well and reward is inevitable and on its way. If not, the next time we do not do it for her as her brain does know, but it just has to search its memory banks for the process. Now we politely suggest, allude to and hint. This approach forces the memory cells to get on board with the habit process. As tutor we should prompt as far as we can go until the learner becomes positively stuck.

If completely stuck, we can swing the pendulum back to guide. We patiently go back to the beginning and show and tell, again and again, repeating who, what, why and where things are, allowing the learner to re-stamp the information into his/her brain and have another

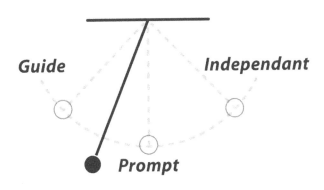

Swing the Pendulum

attempt. Again, with more attempts we can give clear step-by-step instructions and guide, guide, guide. If we are happy that Grandma has got it, we start all over again and let her attempt it on her own. We now swing our teaching pendulum back from guide to prompt. We repeat this process until we are confident that Grandma has got it and can do it on her own. After several promptings we can let her fly and do it by herself. This is now the independent stage.

At this level, we have enough information and skill to enable us to operate the process without guidance or prompt. Here the learner must practice and experiment with our newfound skills and knowledge and cement the learning we need, allowing us to practice on our own without the support of others. This level is independent and the pendulum has swung over to allow the learner to go solo. Our task now, as tutor, is to observe and be on hand if needed. We can swing our pendulum back and forth at any time from independent to guide. Naturally the pendulum must swing through prompt on both occasions as it swings to and fro. It is important to prompt as often as possible. As learning takes time the learner may fall back a little and have to retry with new attempts; by watching from a distance we can intervene at any given time and swing our level of instruction back to guide or prompt until we feel they can go it alone again.

As we have already discussed and seen, we all learn differently and at different speeds. By swinging the pendulum we can interact and react appropriately by swinging from the left (guiding) to prompting in the centre ground and to independent, to the right, thereby offering the correct level of support. This is swinging the pendulum. When using this method we should never assume that we can allow a learner to move directly from guided through to independent instantly with 100% success. This is why it is referred to as a pendulum. It will swing back and forth from guided to independent levels through the prompt level naturally, until the learning is complete. Eventually the learner will not need any more training on the subject or task and Grandma bombards us with emails when we get home!

Synergy and Synergise

The old saying 'the whole is greater than the sum of its parts' expresses the basic meaning of synergy. In the '90s synergy became a trendy buzzword even though it's actually been around since the 17th century. The idea of synergy was one factor in what became a 'merger mania', where all managers were cramming to get synergy, especially the Americans. Unfortunately, most noble business synergy often turned out to be harder to achieve than to imagine. As we saw in the Honey and Mumford scenario earlier, synergy is the benefit that results when two or more agents work together to achieve something either one couldn't have achieved on its own. It's the concept of the whole being greater than the sum of its parts. I would argue that a very plain to see and extremely common example that we fail to see every day of synergy is married couples. Couples, especially when they become parents, have been synergising for thousands of years. The increased effectiveness that results when two or more people or businesses work together. In management, synergies may be created between management teams, resulting in increased capacity and workflow that was not possible when the teams were working independently. Why does it matter? Well, synergies may be elusive, but they are one of the most important objectives in business. To acquire synergy will result in more efficiency; more efficiency brings higher profitability.

Smarter, not Harder

Once we fully understand the aforementioned Ss and work through them, with practice, we can slowly bring all these tools together and begin to work smarter and not harder. Working hard is all well and good. But are we the tortoise or the hare? We all work very hard and put a lot of energy into what we do, but stopping to fuel up our car and being 10 minutes late for that meeting is far smarter than being an hour late because you had to walk three miles with a jerry can. The chimp in our brain told us it was better to keep driving. This is simple (or maybe not so simple, because the chimp made me do it) time management.

So, in summary, already we have taken a look at ourselves with some self-critical analysis; we have researched how to develop our time management skills through the 'stop, start' process and starting with the end in mind. We have even researched how the brain likes to work and examined the 80-20 rule and looked at sharpening our saw. We recall how our brains like to think simultaneously and sequentially and can help ourselves by training the appropriate part of the brain for certain tasks and thought processing. We have looked at setting out priorities and now have a better understanding of how we like to learn. With this new approach we will often find a better solution or make more rational decisions, thus saving us energy and stress with a better chance of getting things right first time, or at least a better outcome than we may have otherwise got. This also saves us precious time by not wasting time. Being productive with our time is both good and positive, giving us more time to think through the next problems and so on. Working smarter and not harder is key to being successful.

Stretching

So finally, now we have taken a good long, hard look at ourselves and we have learnt a little about how our brain ticks and that taking time out to analyse is all positive stuff. We may now agree that slowing down and using the tools we already have can help us achieve personal goals and targets to make us successful. We can now begin to make better decisions with longer-term plans, for ourselves and, therefore, our staff and teams. Now we have these tools we can ask ourselves if we can use them skilfully. The only way to hone the skills or sharpen our saw is to practice. Practice, practice, practice. Skill up! Imagine if you will the next time a member of staff calls us over for help or to solve a problem. Before we dive in, stop, start! Plan out our approach and strategy. Using the tools we now know we have, could we use this opportunity to coach? Or could this be an appropriate time to show our great hands-on management style? Or is it just a good time to show the team we are supporting by using our listening and understanding skills? If we do not practice, we are not stretching ourselves. If we do not stretch ourselves, we will miss out on these life experiences and miss the opportunities to sharpen that saw.

We will not get things right first time, every time. Wisdom and skill comes at a price. An athlete or racing team never become champions if they are not fully committed to pushing and stretching themselves to the limit. The next time we are called to the trade counter or reception, use the 'stop, start' procedure to form a plan. Now we are brand building. Be careful not to overstretch yourself. If you are ask, do we need help? I always say, you can delegate up as well a down. We should always be on hand to help, but if not, build relationships in our peer group, as there will always be someone more experienced and we are not paid to have all the ideas and solutions.

"To live your life is the rarest gift when others simply exist."

Oscar Wilde

"If you're going to take a leap into somewhere, then you need to leap from somewhere."

Anon

Chapter 2
Staff

Staff

In this world of ever-increasing political correctness and equality, the very word staff can sound a little conceited nowadays and can be viewed by some as incorrect. In many quarters other, softer terms are used, such as colleagues, team members, associates and so on. With respect and being as polite as we can, we will retain the word staff for the purpose of our original text.

People sell to people. People buy from people. This rule is proven over millennia and to understand this we must research it. There has never been an alternative. They ask: what comes first, the chicken or the egg? We just haven't the time for that one, but in plain management language, we know we cannot have one without the other and neither works without the other. However, we have already touched on our most important assets, the variables. Us. Self and staff. People are just that, people, and as humans we must never take for granted or underestimate this fact. To look after yourself and your staff, you must put the chicken before any eggs. We discussed understanding ourselves before we begin to understand others. Now let us see why.

What comes first, sales to buy stock or stock to be sold? It may not matter, as, once we are established, it will become a perpetual cycle and, therefore, slightly academic. We will explore this later, but what is important is that we can use 'all the Ss' and understand the interactions and effects that one has on the other. No stock, no sales. No staff, no stock, no standards and no service. No sales, no shrinkage and so on. However, let us try to put the horse before the cart, because everything we do and everything we are revolves around people and our successes depend so much on others as well as ourselves and, as we too are in that same group, it may be correct to draw a line in the sand from the outset. Your number one priority should be people, self and staff. They are and always will be your number one resource and quite possibly the most fluid (variable) resource you will ever have. As a career manager, you will spend your whole working life learning this subject.

This subject is crucial to the survival of, well, everything. The only reason we have commerce, finance, manufacturing, building and retail is because of people. It's that simple. People sell and buy to and from people, so it follows that you need good people around you to support your aims, ambitions and goals. Good staff are not so hard to find and people can be changed through trust and empowerment. Look after them and nurture them and trust them as they will you and you will enjoy their support on your journey. We humans live our lives tending to work on principles. One of our main guiding principles in life is trust, albeit at different levels. Trust is exactly what it is on any particular day and we learn to strengthen it as we build relationships, but through rash or hasty behaviour we can weaken or ruin that trust we spent so long building. Unlike parents or family, work relationship trust has to be earned, so as a manager it is vital that every day we learn to be calm, meticulous, controlled and organised. The more organised you are, the less likely you are to have brush ups or run ins with your staff and we then begin to manage the trust you have worked hard to earn.

To demonstrate a starting point, it may be helpful to assume we are opening a new branch or department within the firm we are working for or setting up our own business for the first time. Where would we start? Since initially we cannot put out stock or sell or offer customer service and so on without a team. People then, or staff, is a great place to start, but when dealing with people always 'expect the unexpected and never assume the obvious'. People are very different, so never be alarmed by other people's decisions or actions. They are not you and probably will not have the same outlook, training or experience as you have. Also people go to work for different reasons and may not be as passionate as you are. Remember we are all different and your knowledge is power.

Seek First to Understand

Dr S Covey, a famous life experience guru, once said, "Seek first to understand before being understood." Here we can suggest we get to know our team first.

What do they need and want? What is their under-standing of the 50-50 contract? They may not see their obligations as clearly as we do, so seek to understand them first. This can avoid tedious and lengthy games of contractual poker and will allow us to get stuck in and check that the company has fulfilled all its contractual obligations and treat the team or workforce with human dignity. Be patient and benevolent, as its rewards are well proven. We can look at our side of the contract later, but in order to make positive headway we should acknowledge that we cannot sell a product to the consumer if it is incomplete or without warranty.

My first lessons in first principles came from an excellent and superbly experienced manager who enjoyed indulg-ing me in my learning and constant questioning. His answers to so many of my questions were often the same. "When you have sat in an employment tribunal for several days you will understand the importance of getting first principles right, the first time around." He was definitely old school and I'm sure he was not aware of Maslow's law. He just called his acts and behaviour decent, moral obligations and first principles, but it is here that I really began to get a better understanding of Maslow's principles and its hierarchy of needs, much more. I later realised that it was here too that I also learnt the true meaning of Isaac Newton's famous quote. "If you can see further than others, then it is because you stand on the shoulders of giants." From the outset, in the very earliest days of our engagement we should consider applying Maslow's theories by looking at your people, staff or teams' very basic needs. Once we fully understand and buy into the 50-50 contract principle we can begin to develop a two-way contract with conviction.

The measure of good management will always be that of what we give to our teams. Give our time, our energy, our respect and our support, but do not feel our efforts create only a one-way street. As mentioned, the contract of engagement will outline what superiors' and subordinates' responsibilities are. If we follow Maslow's rules and are professional, friendly and courteous at all times, we have fulfilled our part of the bargain. There are claw backs and staff are expected to perform at a certain level and standard. Here we will have already outlined those standards from the company policies or through reasonable requests. We do have safeguards. If we have performance managed our teams and individuals still feel we are not getting our share of half of the contract, work through appraisal and review plans. If we say we will review someone's performance in a month's time, make sure we do. If we are on holiday, ask a peer, boss or colleague to do it for us or reappoint the meeting. We must follow through on these issues to maintain our stamp on our branding. Performance management is a very serious issue and should not be taken lightly. Setting performance targets and reviewing is critical to the process and a PPP (personal performance plan) or PIP (personal improvement plan) may be needed. Here we should always show kindness, understanding and real empathy and give staff time for readjustment. Remember it will be easier, quicker and cheaper to retrain than to recruit. Remember, *retrain or recruit*? You decide. If we passionately focus time on a member of staff, our whole team will see that we are a person of our word and that we really are trying with that individual. The team will see and come to understand what it is we are trying to do. Involve supervisors and team leaders to help manage poor performance. This will encourage team buy in, enforce team and peer pressure and, therefore, increase support. Make sure each staff member has involvement. Should the outcome be negative, you will have solid, accurate and concise records to show that you have tried all types of development routes and just maybe that individual was not right for the said environment. In the past I have even gone to the trouble of moving staff to other departments and branches to see if a change in environment can help. It is good to remember that we always have options, so never feel that the two-way street is choked up at one end.

Stakeholders or Shareholders

Before we look at tools that assist us, the mangers of people, we should first recognise that within any business we have both stakeholders and shareholders and we should spend a moment to analyse and understand the two. Shareholders are always stakeholders in a business, but stakeholders are not always shareholders. Arguably, the more important of the two are the stakeholders, who are individuals or groups of people who have an active stake or interest in our business and in the performance of that company for reasons other than sales or stock performance. These groups could be staff (including management), customers, investors, suppliers, communities and even government. But generally in people management, stakeholders are viewed as employees and staff. These are the groups that possibly have the most at stake and the most to lose should things go wrong. Staff dedicate their whole working days, weeks and lives into the one activity of delivering their labour to the good of that business. People, as stakeholders, generally suffer the most when things go wrong and have the most to lose, as in their jobs, their incomes and, therefore, their pension plans, mortgages and houses. It is, therefore, critical, in my view, that we understand and recognise that staff are our biggest stakeholders.

Shareholders should be treated and referred to with similar importance; however, for the purpose of our exercise, shareholders are generally financiers and investors who require a return on their investments, but more than likely have protected their investments by spreading and hedging their bets to minimise any risk. A shareholder would have a share in the stock, wealth and overall returns of the business.

Status Rule

Initially we should never expect more than our status, badge or title might award us. By default our position in the business or company does demand at least some respect, but that is probably about it and, when dealing with staff, initially the best we should aim for is approximately 50%. The rest we will have to earn. If we feel we have to constantly explain we are the boss, chances are our team does not see us as so. Fifty percent respect is the absolute minimum a member of staff can get away with, knowing that they do have certain obligations toward us and our role. They must be polite, courteous and respectful and show some work effort and ethics, but they may move about their roles reluctantly or awkwardly, not wanting to support or partake or, as we say, not 'give 100%.' Here we will have an uphill struggle and we would all rather tow a truck with a good strong team than on our own. Whilst running my own business, an experienced associate once told me: "No one will ever be as passionate about your own personal business as you. So don't expect your staff to be." This is true also for enthusiastic managers, keen to develop themselves. They will have a different outlook and perception on the business to their staff. By using the status rule, we can take comfort knowing that at least we are not starting from scratch, but from 50%. However, the rest is down to us.

Split Rule

Another rule is the 50-50 or split rule and it is worth exploring from the outset. This is the contract we agree on when an employee signs when they begin work. Everyone understands meeting halfway or 50-50 or a two-way street arrangement. Managers and colleagues can often forget that work relationships are just that, a two-way street. You scratch my back and I will scratch yours. "What's in it for me?" This has been the backbone of employment interaction for generations. Ancient history shows us that retail, market stalls and ancient travellers all traded one thing for another. Nothing was entirely free. Retail law is a great example here, as the retailer agrees to sell a certain product, which claims to do this, that or the other, for a set period of time and at a set price. If not, a return, exchange or refund can be awarded to cancel the contract. However, in return the consumer (customer) agrees to pay the required set amount and not to abuse that product beyond its claimed parameters for the said agreed timescale (warranty period). Here lies the initial trust. Once both parties have fulfilled these acts, the contract is complete, but only then is the legal contract fulfilled and complete. Today modern work contracts are the same and are just that; contracts, legally binding two-way agreements, for some form of a return or reward. Also worth taking into consideration is to remind ourselves that very few people sign a work contract because they want to. It is usually because they need to.

Like the retail law contracts, staff employment contracts offer something, explain and agree what the company wants and will do to get it and what the staff member wants and will do in return. These contracts are the absolute basics that should be adhered to at all times. A working contract should always be a two-way street and contain 50-50 participation. If one party feels they are giving more than they are getting, problems and issues will arise. As long as the split rule remains at the 50-50 mark, criticism can be difficult to administer. Explain to staff that you understand their point of view, then prove it and make a little public fuss over it. Make a point of getting staff home on time or even a little earlier, or paying them back a petty cash purchase promptly. In front of others, ask, "Have you had your expenses paid yet?" If not, do it there and then and confirm that it has been actioned. These small acts carry a lot of weight, remembering that staff may not be at our workplace for the same reasons as you. We may absolutely love our job, but the secretary may be there because he or she cannot find a position that they really want or enjoy. We spoke about measuring success in different ways. We all work for different reasons. Also worth remembering is that staff are our customers too via the very contract they signed and out of their efforts, productivity or sales success will come our wages. We have a responsibility and moral obligation to treat them fairly and courteously and with the same respect we would request from them. If we have not kept our side of the bargain, we have failed the 50-50 rule and left ourselves wide open to criticism and even legal procedures.

Sympathy Management

In Monty Python's comedy movie, *The Life of Brian*, the uprising peasants shouted to a village elder, "What have the Romans ever done for us?" The reply from the elder was, "Err... education." The peasants shouted back, "Okay, apart from that." The elder retorted, "Err... sanitary and sewerage systems and clean drinking water." The disgruntled peasants persisted, "All right, apart from education, sanitary and sewerage systems and clean drinking water, what have they ever done for us?" The argument continued. The village elder insisted, "Street lighting, security patrols, safe to walk the streets at night." The rebels conceded, "Okay, but apart from education, sanitary and sewerage systems and clean drinking water, street lighting, security patrols and safe to walk the streets at night, apart from all that, what have the Romans ever done for us?" The crowd thought a moment, then jeered, "Nothing, absolutely nothing." They all cried. How many managers have felt this and possibly suffered in this way? How quickly the disaffected forget. How quickly people become disenfranchised and so easily look for the negatives if its suits their cause. We can never guarantee how people will remember us or think of us, but if we stick to the 50-50 principle at least we will have fulfilled our legal, moral and employment contract with our teams. At least we can walk tall in the confidence that we did our very best to support, help or develop and in a fair and even way.

Sympathy and Empathy

When dealing with people and their feelings, especially team colleagues and work associates, it is always prudent to understand the difference between the two and, with leadership, social and business benefits, once we understand the difference we can apply, where appropriate, the correct approach to help integrate us closer to our teams. Sympathy is where we can listen intently and assure the other party that we value their feelings and we wish to understand, but allowing us to maintain a safe psychological and emotional distance. Bereavement in a colleague's family, for example, would force us to stop, think and make special provisions for that colleague, allowing all parties to spend more time reflecting and consoling. Empathy is often understood to be a deeper emotional expression that links us much closer psychologically and emotionally, possibly if we have experienced a similar emotional feeling and can really, fully understand how that scenario feels. Here perhaps, depression in a colleague is best dealt with by a member of the management team who has also suffered depression. Here that manager can really empathise with the work colleague.

Shifts in Power

Once we understand the split rule and the status rule, we can now begin to develop our management skills as we reflect on shifts in power. Here, when we discuss shifts in power, we really mean horse trading. As we have discussed, many colleagues are only in the job because they have to be and others, even if they want to be, will see the benefits of trading and that age-old question: "What's in it for me?" Why should I start increasing my level of respect for you as my manager? Or why should I improve my commitment to the job or task? Why should I put more effort and quality into my performance, or why should I improve my sales results? These questions are often asked by our teams, although generally not in public. The point here is that we will need more buy in and productivity from our people if we are to improve our own performances and results and we will only get this through our teams. So now we need to trade or even haggle and, whilst looking to succeed, we may have to compromise for a win-win outcome and here there will inevitably be some shifts in power. To engage in this activity we must be confident and ready to let go a little and relinquish some authority, control or even knowledge. To get what we want we may have to let the staff or teams be in control some-times. Ultimately, though, we will have control, for as managers it will always be our prerogative to continue or cease this practice, so we must never feel that all is lost. The best way to navigate this system of motivation is to offer small amounts of trust, authority, control and empowerment to selected individuals at selected times. This way, we are still ultimately in charge of the given situation, but allowing the colleagues to feel that they are now of more importance and you have traded more trust and control over to them to allow them faith to get on with things and deliver more, but on their terms. As managers, we should always be looking to offer our staff something in the way of bartering chips.

Staff Psyche

We agree that we are all different and have different traits as individuals. To help us understand this a little more, we could explore the work of professor L Goldberg in personality assessments. Although he did not create this hypothesis, he is attributed to developing it to today's form and giving it a name: 'OCEAN' or 'the Big 5'. Here he identifies that we as humans all present five (varying levels) traits of personality. Openness, with a willingness to try experiences and new things with a liking for art, ideas, adventure, curiosity and so on. Conscientiousness, with a tendency to want to be organised, self-disciplined, dutiful and reliable. Extraversion, meaning sociable, energetic, assertive and talkative. Agreeableness; identifies us as cooperative, team workers, trusting and helpful. Finally, neuroticism, but in a sense of vulnerability, emotional with feelings and anxiety. Understanding and accepting this 'Big 5' or 'OCEAN' model can remind us managers when dealing with staff that negotiation, listening, trading and selling may be the tools required to assist us in our team development and that we must not use a one size fits all approach.

Succession Planning

Succession planning is also part of the self process and has been around for quite some time. In the early days it was known as talent pool management or company bench strength. As time went by and HR departments developed, the wording was shifted and softened, with emphasis made more positive toward the people rather than that of the company. The practice has been around for a long time and expanded in the early '70s, but today the practice is about our people and teams and how we develop and train them. Succession planning is a process whereby an organisation ensures that employees are recruited and developed to fill each key role within the company. Through the succession planning process, we recruit superior employees, develop their knowledge, skills and abilities to enable them to become multi-skilled and cover numerous roles for the good of the company and prepare them for advancement or promotion into ever more challenging roles. Actively pursuing succession planning can ensure that employees are constantly developed to fill each needed role as they become vacant and, therefore, prevent a problematic panic approach to staffing levels.

Staff Performance

'Can't do or won't do?' is the question we should ask ourselves when it comes to staff performance management. Before we write off staff we should always look to identify the cause and effect. Very often we can be proved so wrong. Believe it or not, it is usually 'can't do' rather than 'won't do'. A lack of knowledge, skill, experience or confidence can prevent an individual from performing to the required standards. If we use the skills already discussed and covered, we can begin to rebuild and fix the problem. People generally see the two-way 50-50 contract obligation and will, therefore, wish to comply. Very rarely is there a belligerent case of won't comply. If there are hurdles and obstacles, these can be increased in size and hidden behind, which then falsely expresses a 'won't do', which only exasperates the problem. But if we look for a cause we will see clearer that the 'can't do' problem supersedes and is the root problem. With a clear understanding we can then search for the hurdles and barriers and then begin to remove them steadily, with training and coaching, one by one, to help the individual or indeed team perform to a better standard. But again the two-way contract always remains in force. If barriers and hurdles are being used to shelter behind, another great saying comes into play. "Can't means won't try." If the 'can't' is a genuine attempt to *not try*, the spirit of the game is eroded and the two-way contract is being abused. If the latter is proven to be true, performance management can again be implemented to the letter to restore a healthier 50-50 balance.

Standards of Performance

If staff performance is becoming a struggle and we have exercised, if not exhausted the split rule with an individual, we will have shown a genuine will to remove the 'can't do' and the 'won't do' barriers. If this is the case, we can correctly assume that the spirit of the agreement has been broken and, therefore, a breech in contract. Should this occur, we do have tools with which to deal with such cases. In these events it is absolutely imperative that we make management notes and document all that is said and done to help any individual who shows resistance to change. Using the Four M formula, we can measure, monitor, manage and then mature that staff performance in a last bid attempt to bring it back on course. By diarising and documenting all that we do, we will build up a strong case to support our requests and demonstrate we have tried all we can to nurture and coach the behaviour. Should this approach fail, we can move to a specific performance management scheme.

Support for Personal Improvement Plan (PIP)

If you have a HR department, liaising with it will help you maintain your professional standards and behaviour to avoid any repercussions, as this is a delicate subject if you are unfamiliar or lack experience. A personal improvement plan is a last chance schedule or programme for staff who cannot or will not conform to the company's performance standards. With HR support (or if you run your own firm there are specialist companies and employment solicitors that can advise), placing staff on a PIP will have one of two outcomes: improvement or parting company. It is worth remembering that some people just may not be up to the job and were fortunate during the recruitment phase. Using a gap analysis, the staff member will be reminded of their 50-50 employment contract and on a strict timescale of objectives (with agreed review dates) they can be retrained to the required job spec standard or mangers requirement, with an emphasis on removing absolutely every barrier and given every opportunity to succeed and win. The input for a manger can be quite intense and the process can be lengthy, but the rewards outweigh the input. As management we should go out of our way to support the individual, documenting and recording in detail all assistance and help along the way. This plan is a legal and recognised approach to dealing with underperformance and can be treated as a disciplinary process, ultimately leading to a verbal, written final warning and dismissal. I have rarely used this process, but when I have the individuals have inevitably turned things around into a win-win situation.

Softly, Softly

Whatever we would want or need from our staff, we must always remember that staff are people and we must treat them with the utmost respect and care and, therefore, we must tread softly. Taking our time slowly and carefully will give us much more than if we take a hammer to crack a nut. Once we fully understand how individual and unique we all are, we will see how fragile individual arrangements, agreements and commitments can be. By treading softly, softly and going carefully we give individuals time to adjust, trial and practice new ideas, routines and schedules. For us, our enthusiasm to succeed will push us onward and give us confidence to trial new things. For staff who are not so driven, things take time and if we drive things through too hard we can put people off and disenfranchise them. This then will hamper our endeavours and we will be forced to work with fewer team members than we would want and maximising all our resources is our priority. We must learn to work at a pace that is more suitable to the team rather than ourselves.

Staff Records (Personal Record Files)

Two most important lessons I learnt as I developed was one, get to know your staff and two, always record and document. As an absolute advocate of putting staff first and when taking over new branches or stores, I would focus time and energy getting to know my staff. After a week or so of settling in, I would ask HR for (and make a big fuss over this, so the jungle drums would do their work) all the team's personnel files. I would read through them all thoroughly, sorting out, tidying and separating all old unrequired items. This exercise has several benefits. Firstly (assuming there are some records on each team member) it can be most interesting reading. It can also provide an accurate measure of that individual. Another benefit is to not only extract expired 'warnings' and 'notes of concern', but also an opportunity to add in or make a note of good achievement. Once finished 'tidying' the files I would one by one invite staff to the office for a coffee and an informal meeting where we would open up the file and discuss its contents. I would highlight and hover over good points, including certificates, awards, qualifications, applications, CVs and notes of praise, obviously leaving them in the file. Any old expired negative notes, I would briefly touch on and hand them over to the individual, allowing *them* to dispose of their own documents as they wished. Any current negative items would be discussed and left in the file with a note explaining the discussion. I never used expensive head office printed forms or fancy report sheets. All I ever used were blank pieces of A4. I would simply date, time, subject and underscore it. Then sign and date at the bottom. This exercise demonstrates openness, clarity and friendship and should be sold as an opportunity as a fresh start for all. They also now know that you know how they have behaved previously and that now you too have a measure and understanding of their performance. This is clearly 'laying our stall out' and 'starting as we mean to go on' and is an excellent exercise in developing relationships. Remember, we spoke of those early studies of workers way back in the early 1930s? It showed any worker will respond positively to some form of personal interest and attention. I believe that to hold true even today.

The second important point of this exercise and an excellent learning curve for me was to document and record everything. Weekly performance reviews, good or bad. Behaviour issues, sickness, absence, punctuality, poor attitude and every conversation I thought worthy of noting. Not all staff relationships blossom. We are not knights on white horses to everyone and I always remembered my old boss telling me tales of industrial tribunals. The more documented evidence you have to defend your actions the better and the more records of you struggling to help improve someone's performance and career the better. I have only ever suffered once in my career and had one real bad apple staff member push me 'to the edge' and into an investigation. Believe me it is not comfortable and a very unpleasant experience. Luckily, events clearly documented over an 18-month period for all to see showed that I had tried and tried to help turn this individual around. As a US prosecutor of the Titanic sinking inquiry once said, referencing the ship's build quality: "Let the record speak for itself."

Safety Cushions

Following on from the last item brings me to safety cushions or corporate cushions. Life in the management fast lane can be extremely hazardous with performance outputs and delivering to target becoming harder and harder these days. Managers are under more and more pressure to perform and a careless, hope and pray approach is one, unprofessional and two, risking your career to chance. Building a good team around us and making the right decision every day is paramount and leaving ourselves open to criticism is asking for trouble. Carrying underperformers, accepting poor standards and being lackadaisical will not do us any favours. We should protect our investment. We have invested hard in becoming who we are, so we should seek to look after it. To protect myself I always thought 'corporate cushions' to guard my derriere! I always pictured in my mind tying a safety cushion to my behind so a kick from my boss or higher would never be a fatal blow. A corporate cushion is simply a policy or procedure. This would mean that all my actions were pre-empted and I had, to the best of my knowledge, followed company protocol and even when pushing the envelope I had a margin of error to work within. This would include things like never turning a blind eye, never accepting second best, never letting staff take advantage, never allowing myself to be compromised and never putting on staff or expecting too much from them, etc. We should always think safety first!

The Seven Ss to Maslow's Law

To establish the split rule starting point we should initially analyse the first principle in Maslow's first law. Firstly, we assess the physiological needs of our staff. These are the physical requirements needed for a human being able to function in a place of work. If we quote quite literally from Maslow, it will be our responsibility to ensure people have ample air, water and food, clothing and shelter. You may query this and feel it a little extreme and silly, but in a workplace people need good ventilation and plenty of fresh air, with clean, fresh running water and a clean eating area with enough time to eat. Consider contractors in your building making a mess, cutting stone or concrete with machines and creating clouds of dust or leaving toxic chemicals or paints lying around. Common sense is not always as obvious as we think. Coupled with this, staff will most likely need appropriate work wear and very often the absolute minimum of correct personal protective equipment (PPE). Are our teams warm and dry in seasonal conditions; do they have quality toilet facilities where they can wash and dry their hands? Do they have adequate loo roll? Do they have soap and nail brushes? Providing all this might seem obvious to some, but many inexperienced managers do not see these items as their priority or indeed concern. We may even be reading this thinking, "Well, I have more important problems to deal with like getting staff to do what they are told or getting staff to be more proactive." I would have to agree, to a degree, but we have obligations and contracts to adhere to. We also need to look at selling concepts. We should sell the benefits, not the features and starting at the front of the problem and not the rear, here comes the example.

Back in the late '90s when nearly everyone smoked and it was still socially acceptable (but not in the canteens) I joined a well-known national supermarket chain. The one building in question employed more than 250 staff members and back in the day most people smoked. On my first day on the job, as I arrived, it was raining hard. After parking my car and running to the staff entrance, jumping ridiculously huge puddles, I noticed many staff on their breaks stood smoking in the bike sheds, but getting absolutely soaked. The reason was the plastic roofs of the bike sheds had never been maintained and consequently provided no shelter whatsoever. Neither had the contract for drain maintenance been managed; therefore, the firm responsible for both issues was invoicing my company, but not turning up to do the work. My very first job that day was to quietly organise a different smoking area until I got the bicycle sheds repaired for the smokers and all the drains unblocked so all staff could walk and not swim to their cars. Quietly, over time, tired uniforms were replaced, toilets and canteens deep cleaned, overtime and holiday pay corrected and paid promptly and time off in lieu for domestic issues granted. The benefit was that staff slowly began to link these 'acts of kindnesses' to my recent arrival, but, unaware of my moral and legal obligations to provide certain services to my team, they began to think I was Santa Claus.

I also quickly learnt that sometimes it is better to take first, then explain it away later (a little overspend here and there) and not wait around to be asked or waste time lobbying. However, do tread carefully with this practice, as asking forgiveness, not permission, can be politically damaging at times and you should always have good justification for your actions. So my first principle, as with Maslow's, shows that we must provide all the basics services to support the human physiological needs.

Maslow's Hierarchy of Needs

The second tier of Maslow's theories is safety needs. Do your staff members feel safe whilst working for your teams? Again common sense should prevail, but it may not be so obvious. We have spoken already about safety equipment, but it is much more than this. This second level includes personal security, financial security, health and well-being (first principle) and a safety net against paid illness or accidents or other problems. Do we, can we and does our company provide financial safety? Is there a pension fund or a share save fund? Are staff eligible, are they aware of them and would they like to join them? Even as a small company director I often brought in an independent financial advisor, in work time, to offer my small team of eight staff free advice and some financial planning. Is there a safe environment for staff to freely express themselves or offer ideas? It may be that the previous managers stifled suggestions or freedom to engage. I knew of one company where staff refused to use their canteen, as the management were always in there too trying too hard to be friendly. The staff felt they could not freely and safely discuss or debate any of the business. There could have been bullying in the workplace or corruption prior to your posting. Do we need to create a safe environment both physically and psychologically? If so, we will have to investigate further and produce a plan. In one company I questioned why one branch had so many rucksack and bags lying all over the floors, potentially causing trip hazards. I commented, "It looks like a kids' school locker room." The reply was it couldn't possibly look like a locker room as there are no lockers and no coat hooks. That was the problem. Staff were not being provided with lockers whilst at work; hence, the untidy and dangerous problem of bags strewn all over. This revelation came from another golden rule of mine. Walk your business. There should be absolutely zero 'no-go areas'. If we do not walk our business we are doing ourselves, our staff and our customers an injustice. It is so important that we see the business from both our employees and our customers' point of view. How can we really begin to understand workers' conditions and environments if we never leave our office? Some managers and sometimes even whole chains of commands are so focused on sales, selling and productivity that they lose sight of what actually delivers all these positive financial gains. The whole team of staff, the workers, the administrators, cleaners, housekeepers and caterers who all support and look after the sellers. So many inexperienced or sometimes selfish managers favour only the sales teams and dismiss or at least neglect the support departments that are actually the backbone of that business.

Another time I remember, I sat in a customer waiting area of a very well-known and prestigious motor car marque dealership, waiting for a meeting with some managers. I sat happily waiting and soon began chatting to a cleaning lady who was wanting to vacuum that room. We chatted and chatted. She offered me coffee and told me it was her double anniversary. During my meeting I asked the two young enthusiastic recruitment and sales managers if they knew of their cleaner's anniversary. Today she was 63 years old and that on the very same day she had also been working at the dealership for 25 years. During the meeting I discovered the two managers did not even know her name. I later sent her a birthday card and asked the management to pass it on to her.

My point here is that it can be so easy to forget some of our people in the enthusiastic and needy drive to win sales. I have known cleaners who have brought sales to a business. All cleaners have families and friends and they too need to purchase items. At a well-known national grocery firm I knew of staff who refused to shop in house because of their poor treatment in the past. I used to say if you really want to know what's going on, ask the cleaners; otherwise, we will always be the last to know. So walk the walk. Walk your business or department. Locker rooms, toilets, smoke areas, boiler rooms and so on. These areas are where your staff work and frequent. And, if only from a health and safety perspective, understand that the whole building or department, as a manager, is probably at least in part our responsibility. These issues must be managed and monitored and constantly maintained. As we develop through our business or career we will learn to delegate to others and to maintain. But always take time to walk your business. 'Walk the walk' as the Americans say. Even after delegating these tasks and roles it will still be part of our operation to monitor and review periodically and ensure that all facilities and services are provided for properly, especially if we wish to maintain good working relationships with our teams.

Once we have fulfilled our social, moral and legal obligations of tiers one and two, after the physiological and safety needs are fulfilled, we can begin to develop tier three of the hierarchy and, as we do, so we begin to fulfil our part of the contract. Next up is love, belonging and worth within the workplace. This third level of human needs is interpersonal and involves feelings of belonging, friendship and family. Humans need to feel a sense of belonging and acceptance among their social groups, regardless of whether these groups are large or small. For example, some larger workforces may include clubs, co-workers, religious groups, professional organisations, sports teams and gangs. Some examples of small social connections include family members, intimate partners, mentors, colleagues and confidants. As we have seen, workers can become susceptible to isolation where there is an absence of this sense of love or belonging element. This need for belonging may overcome the physiological and security needs, depending on the strength of the individual and/or peer pressure. This can be a very good reason for high staff turnover, where staff feel it better for them to move on to pastures new where they will feel more valued. Would we rather be bogged down in a long recruitment drive for weeks on end with fewer staff or would it be better to carry on with full complement, developing, for now at least, with staff we currently have?

To minimise the problems already discussed, the fourth level of Maslow's law and our staff needs are categorised as esteem. Self-esteem, self-confidence, achievement, respect of others and respect by others are all human needs to feel respected. Esteem presents the typical human desire to be accepted and valued by others. People often engage in a profession or hobby to gain recognition. These activities give the person a sense of contribution or value. As a manager it is a positive move to recognise these signs and facilitate and nurture the development of individuals to enhance self-esteem. This is very often and easily overcome by offering small parts of trust and empowerment, allowing individuals to be more autonomous and indeed trusted and empowered. Knowledge is power. If you have children, you will have experienced and practiced this many times. So try it with your team members. You will be surprised by what people can achieve given a chance. Low self-esteem or an inferiority complex may result from imbalances during this level in the hierarchy. Some staff may suppress others, for example. People with low self-esteem often need respect from others; some may feel the need to seek fame or glory, therefore suppressing others. However, fame or glory will not help people to build their self-esteem until they accept who they are internally. Psychological imbalances such as depression can hinder the person from obtaining a higher level of self-esteem or self-respect.

Most people have a need for stable self-respect and self-esteem. Maslow noted two versions of esteem needs: a 'lower' version and a 'higher' version. The 'lower' version of esteem is the need for respect from others. This may include a need for status, recognition, fame, prestige and attention. The 'higher' version manifests itself as the need for self-respect. For example, the person may have a need for strength, competence, mastery, self-confidence, independence and freedom. This 'higher' version takes precedence over the 'lower' version, because it relies on an inner competence established through experience. Deprivation of these needs may lead to an inferiority complex, weakness and helplessness. Maslow states that while he originally thought the needs of humans had strict guidelines, the 'hierarchies are interrelated rather than sharply separated'. This means that esteem and the subsequent levels are not strictly separated; instead, the levels are closely related.

The final level of this hierarchy is what Maslow called self-actualisation. This is the final level, which he believes that once all the previously mentioned levels are achieved the ultimate level is that of a human's morality, creativity, spontaneity, problem-solving, lack of prejudice and the acceptance of facts. Maslow said, "What a man can be, he must be." This quotation forms the basis of the perceived need for self-actualisation. This level of need refers to what a person's full potential is and the realisation of that potential. Maslow describes this level as the desire to accomplish everything that one can, to become the most that one can be. Individuals may perceive or focus on this need very specifically. For example, one individual may have the strong desire to become an ideal parent. In another, the desire may be expressed athletically. For others, it may be expressed in paintings, pictures or inventions. As previously mentioned, Maslow believed that to understand this level of need, the person must not only achieve the previous needs, but also master them.

In his later years, still searching for further explanations to the human will power and drive to move us forward, Maslow explored a further dimension of needs, while criticising his own vision on self-actualisation and called it **self-transcendence.** The self only finds its actualisation in giving itself to some higher goal outside oneself, in altruism and spirituality. As already mentioned, this can possibly be explained by people later in life wanting to become teachers, poets or indeed authors.

To summarise, I would humbly point out, probably unintentionally, Abraham Maslow's research work on his pyramid of human needs is also made up of 'all the Ss' and are all connected rather than separate subjects, with one requiring the support of another. To summarise, Maslow's laws base level of the pyramid is survival; the most basic human need. As managers, only once we have fulfilled the most basic human functions can we understand or fulfil the second tier: safety and security of our people. The need for us and most importantly our staff to feel safe and secure. Once we are successful with these requirements we can then look to the next tier of the pyramid: social needs and a social sense of belonging, wanting to be liked and/or loved and the need to feel wanted or with a sense of belonging in society and within a team. This will include us, the managers, too. We all like to be part of something. The fourth tier is self-esteem. Our and our staff's confidence, achievements, abilities, disciplines, moral compass, comfort zones, self-respect and respect for others, prestige, sense of worth, accomplishments and so on. Finally at the top of the pyramid we have self-actualisation. This simply means us as leaders or any individual team member achieving one's own potential, flowering fully into bloom, reaching our objectives and finding fulfilment, the discovering of our inner talents and creativity, with the acceptance of facts and situations with a solving approach and a lack of prejudices.

Maslows Seven Ss

Abraham Maslow's pyramid of human needs shows us that humans undeniably have absolute different needs and that one need will be prioritised before another. Only when one need is completely fulfilled can we move on to fulfil the next basic need. As managers, it is our role to lift our teams and individuals up the pyramid and support those who wish to rise to the fifth tier, but support those too who struggle or do not crave self-actualisation. We have now completed the life pyramid using all the Ss: survival, safety, security, social and society, self-esteem and self-actualisation. Maslow, through his research and studies, allowed us to understand ourselves and others and identified human needs through clearly categorised and defined labels. Applying 'all the Ss' and 'the Seven Ss' to his methodology, we can now relate to each level through our understanding as good people and business managers. Each level of management need can also be shown clearly in the pyramid diagram. Through his work, we can transfer this learning to 'all the Ss' and by applying his science into our workplace we can see how important, yet how easy these principles sit within a business.

As in life, so too then a business has the very same needs and requirements with each one building on the previous and supporting the latter. Using the Seven Ss, we can see our first tier is *self* and *staff*, the people. A business is absolutely nothing without the people. From the people come the *standards*. The standards at which we are to operate, including systems, policies and procedures and those we and our teams bring into the business. Our morals, housekeeping, punctuality, presentation, attendance and a will to do a good job. Once we have these basic ingredients we need something to sell or trade. Our *stock*. It could be a service or a product, a haircut or a computer programme or just good old-fashioned boxes on a shelf. Understanding our stock and combined with great presentation and housekeeping skills we can move on to the *sales* process. Here we need to manage the supply and availability through our service levels, work on our sales, but protect all our efforts from *shrinkage* and profit erosion. Our last but most important task is to bring all these areas together to manage our offer of *service*. Having got the basics right first time, we can now offer true world-class customer service.

When the time is appropriate, but as early as possible, it is wise to spend time with your teams explaining this

The Seven Ss Hierarchy

Maslow pyramid model. This will reveal your strategy and show how you wish to operate, in a kind, caring and empathetic way. It clearly demonstrates that you do indeed have a clear and thought-out agenda that they can believe and trust in and also take part in and, therefore, win you support in your objectives and goals. A win-win, as they say.

Shiny Lamps

Whilst developing my own skills over the years I developed several anecdotes and metaphors that helped me see things a little clearer. During my studies one image that stayed with me was that of the huge manufacturing plants of Boeing, or the vast libraries beneath the Russian Politburo or the newest of Chinese car factories, all of which are so large it is easier and more efficient for staff to get about by bicycle. Picture the scene. Hundreds of people scurrying about on bicycles delivering parts, documents, plans, drawings, internal mail, supervising and communicating, all beavering away and dashing from point to point, going about their business, but pedalling the bicycles everywhere. In the vast Chinese car factories of Beijing, for safety, headlamps were introduced to the bicycles and for eco reasons these headlights were powered by dynamo rather than battery. The drive wheel of the dynamo was flicked over, making contact with the front tyre, then as the wheel turned, so too would the dynamo and thereby create the electricity for the lights. The harder they pedalled, the faster they went, which of course speeded up the dynamo drive wheel and the brighter their headlights shone. The downside was if the cyclists became stationary they had no lighting!

Among our teams we will always find different types of staff, all with varying levels of interest, enthusiasm, learning abilities and abilities to change or accept change (I call this pedal power). All staff are cyclists, but within our teams are the people whom I call 'shiny lamps'. These people will enthusiastically pedal away like crazy, going about the workplace with a happy and enthusiastic disposition helping win votes and shining bright. Some lights will shine brighter than others, as we all pedal at different speeds. The moral of the story here is to look after them. Pump up their tyres and oil their chains (don't pull them)! Ensure their gears and brakes work and they clean their headlights. Allow them to cycle freely (explore) around the business. Let them keep pedalling so their lights shine bright! Put bluntly, let their enthusiasm shine through and empower them.

Let us now have a look at how we might engage with our staff. As a manager, what would we need from our people? Ensuring we have enough resources, and that our people are suitably matched and equipped for the tasks ahead. Imagine we are starting a new job next Monday morning. What would our first day look like? Remember, people generally do not like change unless they can see a real and positive impact on them or their role. If we are going to implement change, do it gradually and slowly with staff consent or some 'buy in'. Great sales skills will help you get them to buy in to what we would like by explaining the why and wherefores. Do not underestimate this task, as this is a big one. "Why should we do it? Why are we moving or changing stuff? Why aren't sales as good as they could be? Why do we lose customers to the business over the road?" These are all legitimate questions that will often arise, so do make sure we have some good answers and can explain the benefits of our changes.

Sweet Spot

Aiming for the sweet spot is like finding the Holy Grail. Once we have fully explained and trained our staff using the Maslow theory and when we have held meetings and discussed personal record files, performance, objectives, hopes and reservations and after we have given everything and more that our side of the contract demands and after we have gone over and above the 'call of duty' to help our people grow and develop do we reach the 'sweet spot'. This is the point where we have enfranchised, unshackled and empowered our teams. Only when we have consistently delivered on all we have said and promised and received back an enthusiastic and positive attitude can we say we have reached the sweet spot. This is where we find the optimum co-operation, support and input from all parties. Ourselves and our staff, all wanting to support each other. After we have gone through all we have discussed, this where we find dynamic synergy between our staff and managers. This is where we find our sweet spot.

When striving for any of the aforementioned goals, I learnt very early on in the forces the Six P rule. As a Navy diver back in the day with little communication under water, each man absolutely relied on his colleague for dear life, so we always used the Six Ps. That is to say 'poor planning and preparation produces poor performance'. Such a simple rule holds and needs no further explanation, as it carries such weight. As with everything in life, to achieve good things successfully, we need a good plan and a good plan starts with a SMART analysis. This should be followed by a SWOT analysis and cross-referenced with a SORT analysis. It may seem a little top heavy, but planning is about being thorough and meticulous with carefully conceived ideas and research. If we use these three models together we should be able to present a comprehensive and detailed approach to our plans.

SMART Analysis

There is an inconvenient truth about SMART goals. Everybody says they know SMART, many people claim to use SMART, but few, I feel, really know how to use SMART correctly. It is said of the people who use SMART goals that less than a third of the goals are typically SMART in practice. This is a real pity, because our focus should be on achieving clear goals. Instead, our focus is distracted by incomplete and unclear goals. Unclearly defined goals lead to poor results, confusion and even unproductiveness. It is estimated that 70% of all marketing objectives are incomplete. There is no way the activities related to those objectives contribute positively to the strategic goals. The symptoms of poorly defined objectives are easy to detect in daily life: Teams end up in frequent last-minute meetings going through spreadsheets and emails trying to figure out what the initial goal was in the first place. Not to mention internal discussions about whether the team goals are actually met or not.

When we research SMART it may be noticeable that I have replaced the S word, *specific*, with the word *stretching*. For me, there is a little irony in that any SMART plan should be specific from the outset anyway; otherwise, it will not be a well-prepared SMART plan. Whatever our plan, it should be specific from the outset. We will not get buy in and the support we need if we as managers cannot be specific with our plans. Whatever your project or plan, be specific and crystal clear about it forthwith. Once we have a specific target or plan we can apply the SMART process.

So, firstly we need the project or target to be *stretching*. There will be little reward or development if the objective is too easy and can be achieved in no time at all. This clearly would be a waste of our time and a frivolous exercise with the slightest amount of success for our toil. The plan should be stretching in the sense that it will test all those involved and cause some learning and development to take place. It may require some people to step outside their spheres of comfort and to take bolder steps to achieve things.

Once we have an outline plan or objective and we have chosen something that will be stretching we can now double-check that it is actually *measurable*. Here we can quantify by using the M principle. Measure, monitor, manage, then mature it. First we will have monitored the subject matter and this will now afford us a measure. This will normally be the output of performance. This could be measured in units, time, cost or public opinion, but a measure nonetheless that we can use to gauge.

This brings us to *achievable*. We should at this point check that our plan is, in fact, achievable. It is no use us reaching for the stars only to fall flat on our face before our feet leave the ground. Everything we do or ask absolutely must be achievable; otherwise, we are simply kidding ourselves and making a lot of trouble for ourselves and our teams. If it is not achievable, we will not get the buy in and, therefore, will gain no support from the outset.

When satisfied that we have checked our measures, we should now ensure that the plan is *reasonable, reachable, relevant and realistic.* Again it would be foolhardy and remiss of us to lunge forward with the plan if the whole exercise was flawed by not being realistic. This is a safety precaution to prevent us from fooling ourselves that the project is not doomed from the outset.

Finally the complete exercise requires a date stamp. It needs to be *timely*. Here we can now begin planning out our project with a start time and a carefully chosen finish time. Be careful of enthusiasm, ambition and ego. These emotions can often get the better of us and encourage a false sense of completion time. Always allow a safety margin for completion. Explore all eventualities and factor in possible delays and then add another 10% on top of this for good measure!

SWOT Analysis

The usefulness of a SWOT analysis is not limited to large corporations or organisations. It should be used in any decision-making situation where a specific desired end state or objective is required. It is simply an appraisal to analyse internal and external factors, knowledge, skills and resources that could have an impact on a project, target or objective. We can carry out a SWOT analysis exercise any time, both in conjunction with our self-critical analysis or as part of our planning strategy involving staff and team members for even the smallest of in-house projects. If one hasn't come across this before, do not worry. As we become more familiar with it, we will learn to teach our teams to use it too. SWOT analysis is part of the 'stop, start' strategy and its primary function is to show us where we stand before even preparing a plan. Failing to prepare is without question preparing to fail. This is so true and even the smallest of tasks and projects need a small plan if we wish them to go smoothly and especially if other people are involved. Study the problem first and examine the issue.

First we take a look at our *strengths*. Be positive, but realistic and note down all the strengths we have going for us or the team relating to the issue or project. Once we have identified our strengths we can now write down and list our *weaknesses*. This can be a real toughie, so here we need to dig deep and search a little more and I would urge anyone to look harder. If we do not accept there are weaknesses, we cannot be true to ourselves, our staff or the project and that in itself is a weakness and the start of failure. A positive outcome from finding our weaknesses is that we can then use them and convert them into opportunities. Once we have exhausted these we can move on to and research our *opportunities*. Again embrace anything initially and disregard nothing. Look at every opportunity on its own merits. Sometimes things can be a little out of our reach for now, so be careful not to overstretch, but do give every opportunity a chance. Reflect on it and see if you can make it fit comfortably. If it doesn't fit comfortably first time around on paper, chances are it will probably be a struggle rather than a solution thereafter. There will always be many more opportunities than you initially think, but again keep things real and if it costs a lot of money avoid it. Finally in this SWOT exercise we need to look at our *threats*. What is going to hurt us? Is there competition? What is stopping us? Are there financial constraints? Does it need more people? Do we need permission? For example, sometimes advertising banners require local council planning permission before hanging them. So a simple task of putting up a banner now becomes a headache. What problems can we foresee that will need solutions? This threat exercise is as difficult and as negative as weaknesses, but be bold and identify anything.

Once we have our four lists we can begin to prioritise. Without a list, we have nothing to work on. Do not be tempted to gloss over weaknesses or threats. It is easily done in a haze of enthusiasm and positive thinking, but very often with so much enthusiasm we tend not to see or hear everything we should. The human brain has a clever habit of being quite selective at times, so for best results and successful outcomes, stay open-minded. If we genuinely know of problems, identify them so we can deal with them later in a managed fashion.

Now we have a SWOT analysis; what does it tell us? It should show a balanced view of how to tackle our project. The pros and the cons. Study them well and then search for a specific plan. Involve as many of the team as possible. If team members are not directly involved in the project, involving them will only help to build and cement relationships and communicate our ideas or proposals, visions or goals. Once we have our SWOT analysis we can begin to formulate a plan. The SWOT project was our first step to being a SMART manager. Once again involve your teams as much as you can. Explain the whole process and give them the project in tandem with yours. We can run two exercises by letting the team do their own SWOT and SMART exercises. Later we can compare the two plans, checking if we are in tune with our team or vice versa. Always be aware that staff are not always co-operative at first and will want to see the benefits of working with you rather than for you.

Delegate up

It is important to remember that we should never feel like we are working alone. It's also a good idea and smart to delegate up as well as down. In this instance, I mean discuss with our boss or line manager. What input do they have? Have they had this problem before and if so how did they get around it? What would they do better this time around? What resources did they have, etc.? Ask them to commit some form of resource to your plan. By delegating up in this way we can get buy in and support as well as going public, from peers and line management. By going public we will also gain recognition from methodical, well-planned and executed project work and team development. (We are always working on branding.) However, do remember, failing in public can be massive, so go about our planning carefully and quietly and plan to succeed and not to fail.

SORT Analysis

Finally, to complete our planning and armed with a SWOT and SMART analysis we can now employ a SORT analysis. Assuming we have been specific and honest we can begin to '*sort*' out the challenge or objective using both previous models, but now we can develop a *strategy* with an accurate and clear plan of action. A strategy is not a plan per se. The strategy comes from the resources we have on hand. The strategy is the direction from where a plan will develop based on our SMART and SWOT analyses and resources. If we do not understand this, we may deliver the wrong strategy and consequently not follow through to succeed with the plan. Once a strategy is developed, the planning can be formulated. A well-thought-out and planned strategy is absolutely key to our success and without it we will struggle in how we go about our plan. Next we can clearly identify our *objectives*, defining what it is exactly we wish to achieve. What required outcome we would prefer? Start with the end in mind. What are the parameters of the objective and what is being asked of us and are there certain criteria required and so on? Once established we can then review *resources*. What have we got at our disposal? What do we expect to need? Do we need training to achieve the outcome? What tools are needed? Is there a cost that requires covering and so on? Finally, although this heading is actually a resource in itself, it is listed separately, as *time* is always a resource that requires careful management on its own and ironically is a resource that we always wish for more. Here we need to understand, as with SMART, what the timescales and deadlines are and if the *SO* and *R* are achievable within the given time frame. We should also remember that if our *strategy, objectives* or *resources* change so, too, will our *time*. Whilst developing a strategy for the best possible outcomes it is wise to constantly cross-reference objectives with time against strategy over resources until we have exhausted all options.

Sell it!

Once we have done our SWOT, SMART and SORT we should have an accurate plan. Now we need some buy in from our teams. The more planning, the stronger and more logical the SMART/SORT plan will be. If a plan has good reason and rationale, with common sense and logic people will buy into it. They will see the sense in it and logically agree. If the plan is not thorough we will struggle to sell the concept since we will need to invent and manufacture reason. This has been true of politics over the years and the electorate just refuses to vote for it. With a certain degree of logic we can now confidently encourage our people to take some ownership and responsibility for the forthcoming changes and we encourage participation. Why do we need buy in? Well, I'd rather tow a truck with a team than pull one on my own and some aspects of management is achieving things through the activity or the help of others, so give staff buy in; sell it! Be a great salesperson and sell! If you do not have buy in yourself, you may not feel you have the enthusiasm to sell the project or plan. Also worth remembering, as managers we do not always like what we are asked or instructed to do. Sometimes we have to follow instructions and just implement new tasks or new schemes. Here it is a good idea to remember that we may not agree with the politics of a 'roll out', but we will still be measured on how well we actually roll it out. Our performance to manage will still be under observation. If we immerse ourselves in the company's reasons this will help us understand the importance of selling it correctly to our teams.

Sell Benefits, not Features

At this point I feel it important to understand that we should always sell the benefits of why, not the features of what. With people, it is benefits that sell, not features. This is a great sales technique in itself and has been used for years. Features are a 'what to do' whereas benefits are a 'why to do'. For example, assume we are going to buy a car. Let us assume there are two cars very, very similar on the forecourt at exactly the same age, colour, size, condition, mileage and price. How can we decide which one to purchase? A feature of one of the cars could be that it has five doors instead of three like its neighbour. This is a feature. The feature of having five doors was specifically planned and built into the product by the car maker. That is the design feature. But why should we choose to have five doors? What are the benefits to us? Now we are dealing with 'why to do'. What's in it for us? What are the benefits to us, the buyer? What would we gain from choosing this model? Because we are human, we will choose to do something (buy the car) by reason, motives and conditions. We will explore the possibilities and options that we feel suit our conditions best (and, therefore, things that release endorphins) in order to take advantage of the benefits. In this case it may be that we have children and getting those children in and out of a five-door car is just far easier than the three-door option. Therefore, the benefit of a five-door car is that rear passenger access is easier. This is the benefit. Another feature could be that one car is petrol and the other is diesel. The diesel version will do more miles to a gallon. This is the feature built into the product. The benefit is that, over a set period of time, it may, therefore, be cheaper to run. Imagine your conversation with the car salesman.

He says, "Well sir, it's a five-door."

You reply, "Yep, okay. So what?"

"It also has a sprite little three-cylinder diesel engine."

"Yes, okay, so what?"

And "It has black alloy wheels..."

You guessed it... "So what?"

Another example could be a supermarket offering 'buy one, get one free'. The feature here is that two products are being sold together at a lower price than the two items would normally cost individually. This is the feature built into the product. So why should we choose that offer? The benefit will be that it is simply a cheaper option. In this example, the benefit is a monetary reward. So it is the benefits that drive us toward a decision, not the features. Benefits also have lasting effects on us and as long as the product has them and staff see the benefits of having or doing something in a particular way, they will want to continue to keep up with the features. If it is cheaper to commute on a certain bus route, a person will continue to use that route and enjoy its cheaper benefits. If we can get a child to 'buy in' to the benefits of a tidy room (guaranteed pocket money or more treats), it will make the task so much easier with willing, or more willing participants. So if you are looking for some 'buy in', go slowly and sell the benefits.

What if we are to suggest a reorganising of the office layout? That is a feature of the act or objective. Moving things around are features of your plan. As we have seen, it can be hard to sell to your staff or team just on the features. Remember, people generally do not like change and can quite often prefer the status quo if they have a choice. Selling features is not really going to help you make progress. Before asking for or discussing these features or the types of changes you would like, consider their benefits first. It will make the move so much easier and far more permanent, because people will enjoy the benefit of the reward.

One should always involve staff or the team to help do this exercise at any stage and it would be great to involve them from the outset. Involve them completely. Any sign of covert operations will only cause alienation and resistance. Here you would need to be the perfect salesman.

Stealing Ideas

Steal, beg, pinch and borrow ideas. Remember, it is not your job to have all the ideas. If I can be accused of anything as a younger manager it would possibly be that of an over-enthusiastic thief. Eventually I learnt to stop stealing and just began borrowing. I say borrow because as a younger manager stealing ideas it was okay initially, but slowly I learnt that if you constantly steal ideas, staff quickly catch on to this and it can literally stop team members from offering them up in the future. This leads to the perception that, in our enthusiastic error, we seek the glory that should rightly have been theirs. So when I say one borrows ideas, I mean one allows team members to be part of the idea process openly and suggestions can be pooled, encouraging the team to come up with the ideas. When you move on to a new establishment or a new role you can take that idea with you, thereby borrowing it without causing offence. Get the people to have the big ideas, as they are usually the ones working on that particular product, package or project. The ground troops are the ones who live and breathe these issues every day.

Seek and Search

'Seek and search' simply means do your homework. Success does not just happen. We must make it happen. Prepare yourself and others. Always explain your actions and motives. Dealing with suspicious people is far more difficult than dealing with interested and inquisitive people. Drill down with your questioning and again explain why you are doing things in such a way. Playing a little dumb serves many purposes. One, it removes the perception of being a threat, two it encourages openness and a willingness to help and explain, three you learn more and understand more and four it helps team build relationships, and relationship building demonstrates that we are human and do not have all the answers. When questioning, praise the persons involved and let them know that they are the experts, not you. We should also firstly check in our toolbox. Do we have all the right tools? Have we all the right skills? Is the project within our ability? It is no use putting on an extra cash desk to deal with queues if you do not have any more trained checkout operators. It is far more prudent to consolidate our position and check for the correct staff or train people for the required skills first. Search and ask if you can you borrow staff from elsewhere to help you train and build up a pool or bank of skilled and trained operators. Seek out individuals with the required skills or knowledge. Search for solutions. Every problem is a hurdle to be overcome and straddled with a solution. Look positively for a way to succeed and overcome. By standing back and looking at the bigger picture, things can often be viewed from a very different perspective. They say to sleep on things and in the morning, in the cold light of day things are much clearer and easier to see. Also ask, can you go around, over or under to get the problem solved? Problem-solving is literally searching for solutions and searching through all our options and, therefore, involving as many others as we can.

Storm the Brain

As we have said, you cannot possibly have all the ideas. Brainstorming is often a very effective method for finding solutions and the more brains involved, the more effective the process. Simply write down every idea no matter how silly. "There is no such thing as a stupid idea." As Walt Disney said, "If you can dream it you can do it." If you are involving others, do not criticise or ridicule their efforts as it will stifle their output and you could rob yourself of a golden opportunity or a big bright idea. Facilitate and encourage a flow of spontaneous and random, out of the box suggestions from yourself or group in order to allow yourself to find the best of the bunch. It is important that you write down every idea no matter how ridiculous initially. This is the most important part of the exercise. When we feel we have exhausted all ideas and suggestions, we now have our list. Now we can manage the list and prioritise, separating the stupid from the brilliant. Some ideas may cost too much, some may be unworkable or some may need more research, but work through them all and explore what is doable and what is not. This is brainstorming and allows the best or most appropriate ideas for each situation to bubble up to the surface. Brainstorming is a strength and should be encouraged at every stage.

Self-dependency

We are all born dependant. Any creature or animal is, especially mammals. We all need our parents for that support and security in our very early years. Only after we grow do we feel a need to be independent. As people, we show a great degree of tenacity to be independent so much that, as we become teenagers and adolescents, we almost demand our independence and are willing to fight with our guardians to achieve it. After years of dependency, relying solely on our parents, we suddenly decide we want to be free, to exercise our right to independence. We may move out and rent a flat or we just refuse to conform to the status quo and go our own ways, staying out later and later. Doing so, we move on through life, becoming more and more independent, thinking we know everything or at least more than we really do. However, as we age and mature we wish to share and we feel less inhibited about our knowledge or the lack of it. We feel less foolish and develop a wiser way of thinking and achieving. Slowly, over time with the knowledge and experience we have already gained and with a new courage to ask about newer things, we learn to lean on those younger independent people whom we were once so like. We gradually use these independent people when we need to and we use our own independence also when we need to. And so, we become interdependent. This is where we are most willing to 'swing the pendulum' of dependency. Like the pendulum of guide, prompt and independent, we can now decide how and when to swing the pendulum to achieve our needs. We can freely and easily decide when we want to use our teams or when we feel we can decide things without anyone's input. This is when we begin to reach the standard of leadership.

Sequence Management – The Five Ms

As we have discussed already, management is very much a cyclical and recurrent activity requiring constant vision, strength and stamina to allow us to navigate our way ahead, driving and pushing ourselves, our teams and our business on a daily and often even on an hourly basis. Not only do we continually reset goals and targets, but we must also cycle our way, daily, through myriad ever-changing facts, data, reports, figures and information. To be successful, we need to react flexibly and change whenever things cause us to change. This is basic management and to do this we need to adopt a method that allows us to see clearly. Sequence management is a logical approach to dealing with issues under our control. As managers, we will take an area of our responsibility and monitor (analyse) it in order to manage it. The project could be the number of telephone calls the business receives in an hour in order to assign a team member to deal with it in a better fashion; it could be how long the public park their cars in our private car park, preventing legitimate customers from parking and doing business with us. It could be identifying a series of products not selling too well. It could be a customer complaints problem that we have encountered or just simply good old-fashioned poor sales performance. This method is deployed in a sequence of **monitor, measure, manage, maintain, move and or mature** and repeat. "If we cannot monitor it we cannot measure it. If we cannot measure it we cannot manage it. If we cannot manage it, then we cannot maintain, move, make, massage or mature it. If we cannot maintain (object management) or move, make (process management) then we are not managing." Developing the M rule helped me offer staff a way to picture a constructive framework in their minds to help them identify stages and various elements of supervising. This method also helped speed up the learning time required by allowing staff to understand basic management with the aim of giving them a clear path to managing a small section or department within the business. Giving staff an area of responsibility was always one of my first steps to helping empower and develop an individual, always making sure they had the tools for the job, but only giving them what I thought they could deal with. It can be quite daunting to many if we overload staff with things they are not used to.

Monitor

The first step in solving a problem is recognising that there is one. To be able to manage anything we have to monitor it. If we don't monitor, we have nothing to manage and, therefore, no tangible subject matter to get stuck into. Again, here we see the importance of history and research. What is it we are trying to manage and why? We will not understand the history or source of the problem if we do not research and learn from the past. Monitor means literally to watch, observe and oversee, over a chosen period of time. In today's management, computer-generated reports allow us to check the history over a given time and enable us to research and, of course, analyse. Gathering the facts and data using spreadsheets will help us see the patterns and trends that lead to favourable outcomes (success) and, of course, the less favourable (failure). Once we have begun the monitor process we will begin to gather a real-time understanding of the problem. Whatever the topic, to get a firm grip of the problem or issue, we first need to monitor to establish if there is a need to get further involved. Monitoring could be checking regularly hourly, daily, weekly or quarterly. By monitoring, we will be able to see strengths, weakness, opportunities or threats in the specified area. If we involve our people and teams, explaining the need to monitor, it will give them a sense of purpose. Here is a great opportunity to empower our people. As we have already discussed people like to be involved, included (loved) and given trust and responsibility. Even giving out small parts or sections of responsibility and involvement can have a huge effect on our team's behaviour. No 'hearts and minds war' was ever won by implementing one before the other. They both have to be rolled out simultaneously and kept rolling in an even spread, never one giving way to the other.

Measure

Once you have the monitoring systems in place and time passes on, we can now ask our teams to measure the problem or subject by reporting back at meetings or huddles. Depending on the issue, it is possible that systems or practices may not be in place or that this particular subject has never really been managed closely before. So never be surprised, as it could be a difficult process for some, having to fill in extra forms or document and record things on top of their perceived already busy work-load. Support them and provide a positive environment to stimulate participation. Get them to do the analysis so they can see the results of their own hard work. Let them, or help them, do the maths. Now we are managing. By gathering the required information from monitoring we can now begin to understand it and give the said facts and figures some weighting and sense of priority. We can now place some form of measurement to it. The monitor-ing process allows us to see some history. When driving, perhaps we were constantly being overtaken, honked at or bumped out of the way. So now we have a measure, a gauge and a standard with which to compare. A speed-ometer on our dashboard. With a measuring aid we now can begin to manage, to maintain (object). We should now have a better understanding of where we are coming from and where we should be going and possibly why we seemed to be picked on so much by other motorists. It was probably because we wrongly thought thirty miles per hour was, in fact, only twenty. We can now prioritise, judge and compare accurately. It could be financial, time, hours, percentage, best or worse, lowest, strongest and so on. Once we have decided the units involved we have begun to measure. Measuring something allows us to place performance (management) levels and parameters around the issue. Once we understand the parameters or the framework needed to improve or deal with the problem we can really begin to manage forward, toward success. On a daily basis we all measure things in our lives and, therefore, easily understand the process needed to manage an act or particular actions, but we still need the measurement. We know the law maybe, to drive at thirty miles an hour, but without a speedometer we will never know whether we should speed up or slow down. Imagine a busy town or city where all motorists guess the speed limits! Once we have the measuring tool (the speedometer) we can begin to understand fast, slow, high, low, good, bad and better. With the relevant reports we can decide if we are driving too fast, too slow or indeed erratically over a set period of time.

Manage

Now, with the correct information we can decide where we would like to be, possibly at twenty-nine miles per hour. The target figure of 30mph will be our benchmark and the accepted norm. (Our company, the law, the client or even society will set the required standard. Our job as manager is merely to adhere to the required target and develop the team to work toward it.) Staff can often genuinely and sincerely think they are performing or working (driving) at thirty miles an hour when, in fact, they are bobbing along at twenty. This is because they are not using their speedometer. It may well be that they are unaware that it is, in fact, their job to keep an eye on their speed (work performance). Perhaps they thought it was your job as manager and they need not worry about such matters. Through frequent appraisals, offering our teams individual speedos not only allows them to view for themselves their own speed, but also allows them,

from now on, with some coaching, to measure and monitor and, therefore, manage their own performance. When
we carry out regular appraisals with our teams we are
handing them a speedo and asking them to observe it
regularly so that they may manage their own performance.
This empowering creates trust and dignity within our
teams. Once we highlight the importance of staff managing themselves and being responsible for their own
actions, we are now managing to maintain. This is object
management, as we are not asking for 35 or 40mph.

Maintain

Once we have established this practice of empowerment and our teams begin to enjoy varying degrees of
independence and ownership we are now beginning to
manage. By enforcing this practice we are, by definition,
object managing, which is about maintaining and holding
something in the state it was intended. These subjects
could be, as we have suggested, staffs' performance, data
protection, health and safety or employment laws or
company policies on how and when staff appraisals
should be done, for example. Never do things to prove a
point. That will come later through natural progression.
At this point in the process begin looking for team
players who would enjoy being part of the project, who
would benefit and develop from partaking. Offer out
tasks and roles to anyone who is interested in obtaining
buy in from the outset.

Mature or Move on

Once practices are firmly set in place and running
smoothly and we are object managing (maintaining) we

can begin preparing ourselves for the next phase of sequence managing, which is process. This stage can only work on subjects that can be improved on. For instance, if we have already done a complete price and label check, we can do no more. If we have implemented all statutory obligations, we cannot exceed the law, so these subjects are difficult to surpass and, therefore, cannot be part of the process sequence. Our management role with these topics will always be maintain. Subjects such as bettering last year's sales, however, is a perfect fit. Having a full refit of a business, changing layouts or processing systems, or bringing in higher-skilled staff will be part of the process, because we can improve on, mature or move on from what we had, but only after we achieved the object sequence first. Only when we achieve this stage first can we then move on to process.

Sandwich the Success

As we mentioned earlier, success needs to be managed for more than one reason. It may be obvious not to give your teams a head rush, as constantly pushing at success can sap motivation and force a brain drain of success origins, therefore running out of ideas and then, of course, less success. Too much all at once can be too much to handle and praise can become diluted and, as they say, 'familiarity breeds contempt'. However, maintaining an active and positive ambiance and atmosphere also requires great management and people problems constantly need to be challenged and dealt with proactively. To maintain a positive environment when we need to challenge people, we can sandwich positives between negative criticisms. When we need to

PAUL FITZSIMMONS

give our teams or colleagues feedback it should be done through a managed and controlled system using the sandwich process. The reason for this is to maintain a positive tempo and morale, show an orderly approach and to demonstrate as managers that we are in control of the given situation by drip feeding back the positive and negative. Especially if we are trying to convey negatives into positives. It can be most uncomfortable itemising and discussing negative segments. In order to maintain a team or individual's morale, through carefully thought-out analysis we can identify the problem, but before revealing the said negative topic we can research the team or individuals strengths and, therefore, established positives. Then taking two strong positives we can carefully sandwich them in. So we open with a positive note, then tackle the negative and finally finish on a high or positive note to encourage further positive success or actions.

This method is sometimes known as the 'bullshit' sandwich, as in the past managers have used this method simply to get to the criticism. It suggests that there is no thought or care given to the two positives and that these are casually thrown in to allow the negative to be tackled, therefore rendering them as 'bullshit'.

Straight Line Thinking

The definition of a straight line is the shortest possible route between any two given points. Hardwired from birth and geared for survival, our brains learn very early that to compete and survive we have to think quickly on our feet. To react quickly, our brains re-programme for straight line thinking. As we develop into considerate adults our brains learn how to get from thought A to thought C and it needs to pass through thought B. Thought A is the trigger or the cue (the need or the want). Left alone and especially in comfortable and familiar environments, the brain will find the easiest route or straight line thought process between the neurons. If thought B (the response or action) adds little or no apparent initial value to the reward, the path is naturally shortened for a more direct route. Signals are then given out as instructions or response, leading to thought C (reward) where the outcome is held. Over time the brain learns that this new 'straight line' thought process or straight line thinking is much quicker and gets it to the reward quicker, bypassing thought B. Over time thought B (the reasoning) becomes obsolete and manifests into thought C, leaving only two thought points. A, I want and B, I get.

When we retrain and teach someone, we re-angle the straight line thinking with the third point (repositioning thought B) between the two points, A and C, with more relevant information (the response or how or why to). Through more training and coaching we re-identify point B as it should be and, therefore, reintroduce point C correctly. This is reasoning and the exploring of what action should be taken. How should one go about getting something? This changes the habit and, therefore, the reward or outcome. A good example of achieving this is making someone responsible for his or her actions. The response becomes the responsible. This could be a roommate upsetting everyone by constantly drinking all the milk, which is A-B thinking. (Cue – I

want. Reward – I get.) By explaining how the outcome
of the reward is effecting others negatively, we can reintroduce the third angle or thought; building back up the
complete triangle we can push point B back to where it
should be, making it the reasoning and response to the
cue, and reintroduce point C as the reward. Inserting
constant examples or suggestions of 'think about who
bought the milk', 'you are actually stealing the milk',
'what about everyone else?' or 'have you paid for it?'
and so on, you help point B become the analysis and the
conscious moral point. Once point B is reinstalled,
point C changes and the outcome should be more positive. Changing or realigning point B could be 'think of
others', 'buy your own milk', 'drink more water' or
'simply share more'; this still allows the reward, but
roommates could be happier with thought B (how do I
get) and the milk situation is no longer a problem.

In Diagram 1, we can see there is no real thought process or consequence analysis, just straight line thinking.
The brain just wants to go straight to the reward. Point
A equals 'I want milk' and point B equals 'I get milk'.
The part that is missing is the 'how do I get?' But this
straight line thinking has consequences. For every action
there is a reaction. Now we have other roommates un-
happy with our behaviour, as we are always taking all
the milk and not caring for others. We do not care (or
think about) how we get the milk.

An amazing example of how stubborn (straight line
thinking) we humans can be was shown by 'the sappers'
(mine clearance men) of WWII serving in North Africa.
When given new groundbreaking technology (metal

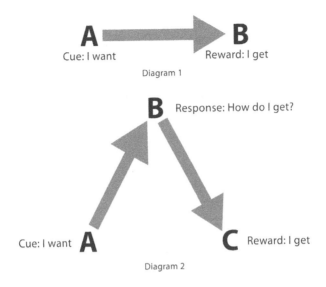

Diagram 1

Diagram 2

Straight-line Thinking

detectors) to help them do their work in a bid to reduce their own deaths and injuries, the men still preferred to use their old faithful bayonets. The men had to be educated (A, B, C thinking) many times before freely abandoning their primitive bayonet methods over the new metal detectors. This example serves only to demonstrate how powerful human habits can be.

The Habit Triangle

They say that a triangle is the strongest shape known in nature and, because of its unique structure, one side always supports another by the way it leans in on itself, thereby supporting at least one other side. We have just looked at building up a triangle to change a habit (move B and insert C). Once the triangle is formed, it will be more difficult to dismantle. The fire triangle is a well-used diagram used in teaching what is needed for a fire to become a fire in the first instance. The diagram also shows that it is impossible to have a fire without one of the three required elements: fuel, heat and oxygen. For a fire to start you need to bring all three together at once. The fuel could be paper, wood, plastic, materials, cloth or a liquid like oil. There is nearly always oxygen around or available, but this can be increased or encouraged in the form of a wind, strong breeze or just a draft. The final element is heat, usually when something gets too hot. When an electrical appliance, for example, has overheated, like curling tongs or a mobile/cell phone on charge for too long. With oxygen in the room or surrounding area, the heat can cause ignition and the plastic in the product begins to melt and burn. Here is our fire. If we remove any one of the three elements, we actually extinguish the fire. This is what the fire extinguisher does. It may pour water on the fire, thereby cooling and removing the heat. It may pour foam on the fire, thereby smothering the blaze and removing the oxygen. We could take a garden rake and claw at the burning cloth or wood, thereby removing the fuel. This is how we dismantle a fire.

Serial Habits

Earlier, we explored learning as being a habit and how we can influence different levels of teaching by 'swinging the pendulum'. As we strive for success to improve and develop our teams, we will find that inevitably much of our work will be in changing people's perceptions and habits. It is most important that we understand how strong the habits of others can be. Serial habits are just that. Habitual and serial by design (or lack of) and not by nature. A bad habit normally occurs due to lack of information or intervention (straight line thinking) and will constantly, predictably, reoccur on a repeated and regular basis.

The Fire Triangle

The Serial Habit Triangle

We often say we have a burning desire. So like the fire triangle a habit requires three elements also for all of its three sides and once complete it too is very difficult to remove or break apart. However, once we begin to remove any one element (or side) the triangle folds or collapses and ceases to be a triangle. Using the same approach, we can form in our minds a habit triangle. The habit is the fire. In the same way we now know a fire can only exist when all three elements are brought together, this too holds true for a habit. As with the fire triangle example, a habit can only form when all three elements converge simultaneously, since one requires the support of the others. Here we have knowledge, skill and desire. If a person does not know what to do (the knowledge), it will be difficult for him or her to habitually do something. Similarly, they may have the skill (the how to do) and the knowledge (the 'what' to do), but they do not have the desire (the 'why' to do). Therefore, the habit (triangle) cannot develop.

Great examples of this are the age-old habits of parents wanting their child's bedroom tidied, smoking or not smoking and overeating or dieting. A person will only develop the habit of smoking once 'the what to' smoke (knowledge) and 'the how to' smoke (skill) are brought together finally with the 'why' (the desire, also known as the want or the need or plain old will power). The want or need (desire) to smoke may only fully change the habit to not smoking (quitting) or dieting when the desire to stop is fully enshrined in the brain. A person may know how to smoke and what to smoke, but has no desire to smoke. Again a person may know what to eat and how to eat, but may have eventually trained the brain to lose the desire to constantly eat. Once the desire has changed the knowledge and skill are just that. Knowledge and skill. Let us look at a child who will not keep his or her bedroom tidy. They will have been told by the parent how to tidy (the knowledge) and they will have been shown (the skill) and then encouraged with treats or pocket money to fold clothes, tidy toys and put things in drawers (the desire), but, unless you can really sell all the benefits and features of a tidy room (change the knowledge), a young person will have little or no desire, unless you offer them gold!

Another view is a person with great desire to do something and who has read up on the matter and gained the knowledge, but has yet to master the activity and develop the skill. It cannot be habit forming until the skill has developed. A learner driver is a perfect example. Passing the mandatory theory test (the knowledge) does not guarantee a practical test pass. The learner driver has to build up the knowledge, then the skill with a desire to pass the test.

The Serial Habit Triangle

To summarise, a habit is a thought process with an act of relevance that *has to become enshrined in the brain and repeated over and over* willingly with all three elements playing their part. The skill, the knowledge and the desire all need to be present to create an effective habit. So then, if, as managers, we wish to establish a habit or good practice and/or remove a bad or poor one, it is important to remember that a habit requires the adjustment of these elements and as part of your leadership and management role it is down to your skill and judgement to identify which element is the best one to replace, remove or enhance. As skills and knowledge are difficult to remove, but not impossible (as retraining can counter this), the easier answer will invariably be… desire. We can change the desire. Change the want or the need. This is where great sales people win their bonuses, company cars or super holidays. They work on and sell to our desires. They change our desires and, therefore, get us to buy into what they are selling. They create desire by enhancing our perception of the want or the need and thereby create a buying habit. But remember it is equally important to work on and develop the skill and knowledge too before we expect too much from our teams. People can have a real desire to do something, but are not yet equipped. This is why it is the habit triangle.

Staff Supply

Getting great staff is hard; in fact, it can be extremely difficult, even exhausting, with a huge drain on our time and resources and making wrong choices can prove to be even harder to undo and can stifle our succession plans and team development. Correcting getting it wrong, although painful, can have positive effects and, by demonstrating firm but fair performance management, our teams will see that we insist on tough or high-quality standards and we will not accept poor performance. Probation periods are crucial to help us get through this initial phase of recruitment and probation periods should be tightly managed to ensure great staff filter through into the mainstream of the business and the not so great are given every opportunity. When you are presented with an opportunity to recruit fresh staff take the 'stop, start' approach and analyse the 'who, what, where and why'. Insist on a clear action plan with a SMART analysis attached to it. It is absolutely crucial to save time and money to get this process right first time. Examine very closely the vacancy itself. Just because someone has left the business does not automatically mean that vacancy should be replaced exactly. Can we work smarter with a different approach to the hours lost? Can the business manage without those hours altogether? Can we incorporate the required gap into other roles or a new type of role established in a cheaper capacity? Remember staff wages will always be your biggest expenditure and affect your 'bottom line' massively, so any chance to reduce those precious overheads should be examined. Staff can leave abruptly within weeks of giving notice, assuming they do give notice. Recruitment campaigns can take months and, therefore, a succession plan is vital to fill, or at least bridge that vacancy gap until you have the right person on board. Once established that we definitely must recruit and replace in some form it means we now need a strategy and a clear plan to get it as absolutely right as possible. That doesn't mean to say that we will be successful first time around. Bear in mind companies spend millions on HR and personnel departments, aimed at delivering great people to the managers, and also remember those same businesses also spend many more thousands again on training once the recruitment process is complete. Therefore, it will pay dividends to analyse the training requirements needed to save or minimise downtime caused by inductions and training.

As we have said, recruitment is a tough game and finding the perfect candidate is easier said than done. Suffice to say your role is to get it as right as you can based on evidence. Some people are very, very convincing at interviews and will sell themselves superbly, but look for hidden history of poor performance. Once a recruitment drive has been decided give it time, lots of it. Fill you fuel tank to the brim with this project. You will only get out what you put in. Delegate where you can, but stay informed and in control.

Short listing

If we do not have the luxury of a head office HR department, try to forge links with the branch manager of our local job or employment centre. He or she can flag listings and prioritise people and resources to push more applicants our way. The wider we cast our net, the better choice of fish. A job centre will normally let us use their offices and telephones, etc. and would usually not charge for these services. They will often help us to shortlist and they can even advise on funded recruitment offering bounties. So before we begin spending large amounts of money on newspaper ads try the simple approach first. Also, if we have tech savvy staff, try social and digital media and posters in our windows and brief our teams at meetings to actively spread the word and recruit for us with perhaps offering them a reward. We should spend our time to organise and diarise after the short listing is complete. Here we will want to interview thoroughly and factually. Do our research to check the short listings are correct and then prepare thoroughly for the interviews. Again if we have experienced juniors whom we can trust to interview, we should delegate to encourage team input. We can have the final say at the second or final interview. Work through, diligently, all possibles and contenders, looking for strong experience, specialities or training with quantified qualifications that are certified. Remember, this can save large amounts of money and time on training should they be successful.

Scheme of Work

We use schemes of work in the UK for teaching. It is a guide that outlines the work required and to what standard with defined structure and content. It maps out clearly how resources, activities and assessment strategies should be used to meet the required outcomes. This is a great tool that is usually an interpretation of a specification or syllabus, but can be used as a guide throughout the probation period to monitor progress against the original plan. Schemes of work should be shared with candidates so that they have an overview of the standards, training and required work schedule. Here the probation period should be highlighted and made absolutely clear to the candidate and that this probation period can be extended if required.

Sales Pitching

Assuming you have successfully appointed a candidate, the interview process is a perfect opportunity to sell the business and our vision for the future, to give and get a clear understanding of the new contract between both parties. From the outset, expectations, standards, hopes and beliefs can be clearly spelt out and explained in simple terms to help us get buy in from the outset. Taking on new recruits, although taxing and stressful, can also be an exciting time building up a new team, forging and developing personalities, ideas and strengths. This period is our best time to reinvigorate and build a fresh team, setting out new goals and ambitions with fresh people on board who have no or little knowledge of the firm's past.

Succession Planning

Having looked at self and staff, we have now established, clearly, that the most important asset to us and our business is our people and our team, and having looked at Maslow's laws in some depth we discussed some of the moral obligations we need. It would surely be prudent, then, to want to care for this asset. As the fables tell us, look after that golden goose and don't bite the hand that feeds us. In our case, we not only need to protect, but to grow and nurture, for good reason. As we know, we humans constantly need checking in on. We grow bored, we lose interest, we can see problems that may not be there and we all suffer from happiness and depression. Some of us are more stable than others are. How, then, can we best motivate, care for and help our teams maintain interest and enthusiasm to aspire?

To look after staff and self, we should use succession planning. Succession planning has been around for quite some time and in the early days was known as talent pool management or company bench strength. As time went by and HR departments developed, the wording was shifted with emphasis made more positive toward the people rather than that of the company. The practice has been around for a long time and expanded in the early '70s, but today the practice is about our people and teams and how we develop and train them. Put simply, succession planning is a process whereby an organisation ensures that employees are recruited and developed to fill each key role within the company. Through the succession planning process, we recruit superior employees, develop their knowledge, skills and abilities, and prepare them for advancement or promotion into ever more challenging roles. Actively pursuing succession planning can ensure that employees are constantly developed to fill each needed role. As your organisation expands, it loses key employees, it provides promotional opportunities and it increases sales. Succession planning guarantees that we have employees on hand ready and waiting to fill new roles. Succession planning increases the availability of capable individuals who are prepared to assume such roles as they become available. Thus, one of the benefits of succession planning is reduced risk associated with a loss of experienced and key workers. For me, it is simply how we look after our people in the work environment.

Through structure, scheduling, schooling, status and supporting, succession planning is how we encourage staff and teams to develop themselves, one to improve and increase their own individual performance to give a higher return to the company, and also to allow them to grow and develop positively into roles, thereby blocking off shortfalls in manpower and production, and secondly to allow individuals confidence and faith in their employers and demonstrate that they are valued. Without pausing to allow for any cynicism we must actively lay out from the outset that we will fulfil our part of the contract and offer teams support, schooling staffing and opportunity for success. Remember the cycle lamps? Keep them pedalling, as they will want to shine bright! To keep them shining bright we need to remember they need support, structure, scheduling and schooling.

Textbook succession planning is a process for identifying and developing our people with the potential to fill key business leadership positions in the company. Succession planning increases the availability of experienced and capable employees who are prepared to assume these roles as they become available. Although I must agree, I feel a horse before the cart moment for me, as people are the key ingredient, people, people, people, and we must look after the golden goose! Working to Maslow's laws and our two-way street, 50-50 contracts, I favour succession planning as a gateway or portal to open up one's full potential and inspire our teams, without ulterior motives such as filling vacancies and emergency planning. If we adopt this approach, we are genuinely fulfilling a moral obligation first, by offering our people a chance to grow and flourish, therefore switching them on, empowering and allowing them to realise potential within their own measurements and remits of success. Only then can we fill the said vacancies. Would it matter if that person moves on to another company, business or department? No, it should not matter, for, if we have adopted a great succession planning approach, that person will take with them, for free, all the great training, teaching and support that we gave and should speak highly of us to our envious competitors.

Staff Rooms

A quick note on staff rooms. I have seen over years of managing that many staff rooms, through ignorance or lack of consideration, are frequently abused by managers. A staff room is and should be just that. A staff room. This is not an area for managers to hang out; neither should it be a place for us to splatter our notices, work information and sales charts. A staff room should be a place for staff to remove themselves from the business. When they enter the staff room it should be a place of rest and relaxation and a place where they can switch off from it all. Of course, space is always an issue and generally speaking planners do not do staff rooms justice. My point here is, where possible, even with the smallest of buildings, make a conscious effort to de-clutter and remove as much work material from the staff room as possible and make it theirs, not ours. This lack of work-related information reaffirms a psychological security and reduces thoughts of corporate oppression. A staff room should not be a stock room or a delivery area. Courier firms and parcel firms should not be encouraged to use a staff room as an easy drop!

Work clutter and equipment should always be removed. If we remember Maslow's laws and the 50-50 rule, it is our job to provide a clean, comfortable warm and safe environment for rest periods. As well as a moral obligation, if there were ever a staff issue or a tribunal, again, these things can bounce back, so keep that safety cushion firmly secured to one's behind! Ideally, the only notices and posters in staff rooms should be what the staff wish to have. We should always give careful thought to staff rooms and always create separate notice boards in communal areas wherever possible. In one establishment, I removed an area of a warehouse and had a canteen built, as the business had failed to provide even the smallest of staff rest area.

KISS

'Keep it simple, stupid' is a well-known phrase. Apparently the story goes that an IT development manager at IBM was trying to gain funding for a project he was working on, which resulted in him giving an ill-prepared presentation to senior managers, including finance managers and accountants who knew much less about computer programmes. Not being the most social creature and lacking confidence, unfamiliar with presentations, he spoke in such a way that he totally baffled and bemused his audience, using only technical jargon, unknown acronyms and general tech geek speak. He automatically viewed his colleagues as stupid, not being able to follow or understand his presentation. The managers were indeed looking at him strangely, but he felt they were all stupid for not understanding him. In a desperate bid to save some grace, he asked his audience why they were all looking at him as if he was dumb. In an attempt to enlighten and diffuse the atmosphere, the chairperson replied, "Keep it simple, stupid." The case in point here is that, in fact, it was the IT geek who was the stupid one. Being too clever for our own good, confusing people, not understanding whom we are working with and having no empathy with our audience will only make us look like the stupid one. The lesson is not only to be clear and concise, but also to keep things as simple as you can. If you want people to buy in quickly and successfully into our requests, instructions or tasks, keep things as simple as possible. Remember that people have to learn and take on board and process what we are asking of them. We always need to bear in mind how our teams learn and what learning styles they have naturally adopted. If our requests are awkward or too complicated and long-winded, our messages will be lost and we will set up ourselves and our people to fail.

Structure building – Planks or Bridges?

By using Maslow's hierarchy model, the serial habit triangle and all the other newfound tools in our toolbox, we are now able to build some structure. This structure is immensely important in shaping the world around us. Through an improved structured approach to our role, we can now focus our energy into driving the business we are managing. When we bring structure to a business we begin to build bridges, permanent routines, policies and practices. This should create a calmer environment where everyone works better, allowing us to tackle more difficult and challenging projects like growing a business. However, we must ensure that we are building permanent solid bridges and not just simply laying out planks. Building bridges means long-term, substantial, concrete processes, routines and practices that become habit forming and difficult to remove. Planks are feeble, ad hoc, loose, temporary, maybe today, maybe tomorrow attempts to organise and manage. Building bridges should be part of our branding and we should be bringing calm and controlled environments to our workplace. This is an excellent measure to our development levels of managing success and branding. I would not suggest that this approach is quick. This can be a very slow process and, like everything, takes time to build. McLaren or Red Bull didn't just become Formula One champions overnight. Every winning team takes years of development, understanding, listening, nurturing and research before it comes to fruition and blossoms.

We should always remember that people are people, which makes us all complex creatures and we as managers are, therefore, not psychologists and can only do so much. It can be hard going at times and certainly frustrating as we pick our way through the maze of management advice, people skills and management tool approaches. And if there is one thing to be sure about, it is that we too are only human. Do not expect to get it right all the time and do not expect to be liked all the time either. We can please some people most of the time, but we cannot please most people all of the time! We must content ourselves with the facts, that we have applied all the Ss and Maslow's law and indulged our teams with real empathy and understanding. If we then have to apply the split 50-50 rules and part company, so be it. We are paid on final end results.

Support, Don't Stifle

To bring this chapter to a close, we should finally observe the rule of 'support, don't stifle'. This rule really is golden. Even through the most difficult of times a good manager will support a team through thick and thin. Support goes further than just work ethics of training and developing. Remembering Maslow's laws, even if staff are struggling in their personal lives we can help support them on an everyday basis. If we have learnt to understand our teams, we will begin to learn their domestic problems also. Here as managers we can step in, offering advice or assistance in many small ways. This can range from allowing them to go early to doctors or dentist, or time off for difficult times, for example, without any penalty. Moving shift patterns to help with bus or train times, car sharing or even 'cycle to work' schemes. Child care and crèche packages can be advantageous to both parent and manager. People with general health problems can be assisted by departmental moves to help improve performance. If we rule with an iron rod, we risk damaging that often fragile 50-50 rule and this results in stifling enthusiasm, ideas and a wish to participate. This can only work against management in the long run. We can always fall back on enforcing the 50-50 rule as a last resort if staff are genuinely taking advantage of our caring, supporting approach. We should not be getting bogged down by petty 'who owes who' disputes over being owed five or 10 minutes. We can bank all these issues, allowing us the grace and dignity of reminding people later should we need to. It is bigger and greater to give than to receive and, as the old saying goes, what goes around comes around... and remembering: "What did the Romans ever do for us?"

Some Alphabetical Formulae

The 4 Ms: Monitor; measure; maintain; move

The 5 Ws: Who; what; when; where; why?

The 6 Ps: Poor planning and preparation provides poor performance

The 7 Ss: Self; staff; standards; stock; sales; shrinkage; service

The 7 Maslow Ss: Survival; safety; security; social and society; self-esteem; self-actualisation

"Chop your own firewood. It'll warm you twice."

Henry Ford

"You will never reach your destination if you stop to throw stones at every dog that barks."

Winston Churchill

Chapter 3
Standards

Standards

We have spent time already looking at the two most indispensable and most important assets in our toolbox. As we can see, these are the only two human elements to 'the Seven Ss' so it should be no surprise that we spend quality time on them. However, by default and by taking a good hard look at ourselves and our moral obligations, we begin to instil standards. If, after some reflection, we now agree that self and staff are worthy of our thoughts and considerations, the understanding, support for and automatic application of standards will come to us much more easily. Only with synchronisation, and synergy with self and staff can we begin to deliver standards.

Moral Compass

To make inroads into the standards around us we must first understand our own set of values and moral compass. The moral compass that we develop over time allows us to see what and why we hold the standards that we do. With thanks to our parents, peers and colleagues, our moral compass will be an internalised set of values and objectives that guide us with regard to ethical behaviour and decision-making. It is a natural feeling that tells us what is right and wrong and how we should behave. It is an inner sense that distinguishes what is right from what is wrong, functioning as a guide (like the needle of a compass) for morally appropriate behaviour. All of us have the foundation for building a strong moral compass and there are many benefits to having this. It gives people a sense of integrity, which is a tool for helping with a sense of self-worth and self-confidence and we too as managers are also driven by Maslow's laws and rules. This sense of self-confidence is not dependent on the outside world, but rather an internal feeling and evidence suggests that people who have a healthy functioning moral compass are more grounded, more focused and more content with life and, therefore, more productive. They also appear to have more nurturing and positive relationships with people around them and their environment. They wish minimum harm to the world and maximise their contributions. In other words, they like and wish to give back as much as they take in, or maybe even more. They also have a healthier sense of individualistic self, while concentrating on a good for all.

We require an individual sense of what it means to be moral. This cannot be emulated. We can learn from others if it makes sense, but we have to build a set of values for ourselves. We may ask ourselves if we are following a set of outdated or skewed beliefs that are counterproductive. If so, why? How do I modify them? What beliefs or standards can we follow? Do we know ourselves enough to know how our beliefs can be shaped for the better? We have to learn to focus on more than the outer appearance of things. Physical standards can be taught or at least seen immediately and, therefore, we can learn them quickly. Phrases such as 'what a good job looks like', for example, can be used easily. Company rules and policies are a great de facto starting point also. Internal standards or morals, however, cannot be seen and, therefore, need to be discussed, explained, passed on and taught. But initially the outer appearance is a great place to start. Especially with how things look to others, as perceptions are important. If things put before us look organised, clean and presentable, they generally are. Also, to get those images or perceptions to the said standards, the systems in place behind the scenes that got them there in the first place are usually in good shape too.

When we try to identify standards, it can often be a struggle. We would usually look to find current operational levels often set out by company procedures, policies or legislation or use previous history. Using these benchmarks, we would build standards around these frameworks or parameters for us to work within. But what standards do we want? What are we trying to achieve? What standards would we like or what indeed should we have? Do we actually need a standard at all? The obvious answer should normally always be yes. In the commercial world of management, we would always be looking to see what standards we have had already and, using the four Ms, we would check our history and then assess the standards we expect to have in the future. As managers, we are always judged, monitored and indeed remembered for our achievements (standards) and this is part of our branding process. This then itself sets a precedent for us and begins to answer the question of what standards we need. Initially from a commercial management standpoint our standards will be guided by sales history, budgets and policy, but the rest should be from the perceptions of others. What do people think of us and how do they see us? Do we project our brand? Do our teams and peers see different standards from that of our predecessors? What is it that sets us aside? How are we different? In the first chapter, we looked at 'self': ourselves. This is where our very first set of standards will come from. From here we can check with ourselves our very own set of standards and decide if our standards can hold up or improve on the past ones. As managers it is natural that we are constantly measured and judged and, therefore, we should always be aware of and then explain this to others and, as a result, we must improve and develop across a range of subjects and areas. To help us identify or structure the question of standards we can use 'the Seven Ss' to help us see where we might wish to be with the development or improvement of them.

Change will not come easy. To improve our own standards takes time and will involve journeys of development and discovery, but if the awareness, will, tenacity and the want for change is there, it will happen. Naturally over time as people, we begin to develop and improve. Quite often too, as we work alongside and observe our peers and superiors we subconsciously develop our styles and behaviours. Quite often we go through life experiences that offer us paradigm shifts and unique views from a different perspective. As we grow and mature, our views, morals and opinions change, even our politics, allowing us to develop and improve our personal standards and finally deliver on our branding.

Having first looked at self, and using self-critical analysis, we can ask what is there about us, our *self*, that we can improve on? We have looked at these subjects already and can now begin to look at ourselves from the outside and understand others' perceptions of us and what standards we have and how we go about our daily lives, how we form relationships and manage and lead others, how we sympathise and empathise with others and so on. As we saw earlier in the previous chapters understanding ourselves and how we operate is the start to understanding everything else, including our own behavioural standards. Once we accept and acknowledge where we are, we can begin to develop and improve on them and, therefore, set the example and lead from the front, showing others what standards are acceptable. This is known as a paradigm shift.

Firstly, we should start by examining our own standards. Do we do what we ask of others? Do we lead from the front and at least try to set good examples? By this we would mean we arrive for work in plenty of time, washed, shaved, well groomed, wearing the correct or appropriate uniform or clothing, which is cleaned, smartly ironed and with footwear clean and polished. This presentational standard is factual, visual, evidence that we really do care and that we can and do go to great lengths to present ourselves well to the public with a high standard. Remember, first impressions count and give off excellent positive vibes. These are some of our basic, primary standards, but become part of our personal branding. What time do we arrive at work? These are the first examples we set and it is no good coming and going in and out of our work as and when we feel like (just because we can), but chastising our teammates for poor punctuality, or pass negative comments on the standard of the restroom or tea room when we never clear up or wash up ourselves. We should not demand of others what we *do not* deliver ourselves. Identifying with any of these types of examples is okay, but we should work on them to improve our personal standards, then pass them on to others where possible. We can now immediately see that we are setting a standard for others to follow. Ask ourselves is our mannerism or demeanour positive once we arrive at work or do we play out the role of a grumpy and tired person who is always bad mannered because we are 'just not morning people'? Again this is a clear and visual message that our teams will pick up on and does nothing to inspire. Do we speak to our teams politely and courteously with good, clear messages? Are we calm and do we show control? Do we command an audience or do we demand an audience? Do we have clear, well-thought-out messages with well-planned requests and instructions? If not, we are setting out down a darker path. It is so important that we ensure these basic standards are in place if we are to command the fullest respect and at the very least generate enthusiasm from teams with the minimum amount of cynicism. We must show our teams that we are trying to be whiter than white. These are the first steps in good leadership. No matter what our company position or title, if we cannot get these basics right, the rest will be a battle. Remembering, the title on our company name badge demands only 50% respect. The rest we have to earn. I used to enjoy the commute to work, as I found this a good time to reflect and gather my thoughts. It allowed me to arrange, prioritise and plan and sort myself for the day or the following day. On my arrival at work I had in my mind a plan for myself that I could implement or at least integrate with anything urgent that may be waiting for me.

Following with the 'the Seven Ss' rule, the next phase, of course, will be standards of others, our teams or our staff. Do they know the standards that are expected, bearing in mind if we are new to the role or have recently taken over, our standards will be different from our predecessors' and teams will need time to adjust? We should use this time to investigate and explore (using our new tools such as the four Ms, 'gap analysis', SWOT, SMART and SORT, etc.) areas for development. This time is what we call the honeymoon period. During this honeymoon period it is good management practice that we agree with our line managers, peers and our team, a reasonable timescale to train and bring up to speed staff with essential company policies, practices and legal obligational standards. We should use this time wisely to organise coaching and training sessions, for policies and standards may have been slack or even missing in the past. We require our common sense and to have open discussions about our findings, then we seek agreements to find a standard that everyone can work toward. When doing this ask ourselves, do we encourage staff to take ownership and responsibility and get involved? Are we flexible and patient and allow for leniency when difficult situations arise?

If we work for a larger more corporate firm, normally the standards will already be in place albeit to differing levels. It will be our job to simply develop them to conform (object managing). Quite often the standards of our bosses become our standards by default. They may demand x or y and, therefore, we have to work a little harder to achieve this. We may have to up our game to reach their standard. Even if we have recently taken over a small business there will be previous sales and purchasing records. These will be our initial standards. It may be sales volume standards, it could be the number of files to be archived, the presentation of stock, or indeed the standard of stock holding, replenishment or the number of customers engaged with. If dealing with people in care homes, say, it could be a record of achievement in delivering a quality of life or a standard of enrichment. Whatever the standard, we must allow all parties involved time to change and develop, including the receiver. Encouraging teams to meet the new standards is part of the management role and helping them to achieve meeting these new standards is of paramount importance. Having high standards is commendable, but they must be achievable and not be at any price. If you are new to your position, as we have already discussed, this will always be an ideal time to implement new standards and introduce better ways or new improved versions. As we have said, returning to work from a vacation or a training course is also a great time to take effective action, or if you have simply just made the decision to change your ways and standards, you are beginning to sow the seeds for future success, so take time to sow what you wish to grow. This is good management and great leadership.

The required standards will be all around us and most required standards will be driven by sales, health and safety, law, finance, budgets and so on, but also from the cleanliness and housekeeping of our offices, to our shops, depots or branches to the presentation of our products, the clarity of our pricing and offer message to the level of stock we carry in order to support our anticipated sales. From the standard of experience and skill level available from our team to the level of customer service and after sales provided. To achieve success, all these areas will need high standards of management. Remember success by definition cannot just simply happen; it has to come by design and development. It is the accomplishment of an aim or a purpose. Success is the fruit of our labour. If we can get standards right, we will begin to succeed.

We all personally favour the use of a clean and hygienic bathroom with quality toilet tissue. We all prefer to wash our hands under hot water rather than freezing cold. When we all smoked at work many years ago, we preferred to do it in the dry of a bike shed and not in the rain. When we go to the stationery cupboard we expect to find what we went for. We would all prefer to eat in a comfortable canteen area rather than sit in our car and, at the end of a hard week or month, we expect to be paid exactly what was promised and on time, with a payslip to prove it and so on. These issues are so fundamental and obvious to civilised society that they are now enshrined in Western European ways and values and even embedded into society through the UKs Health & Safety at Work Act 1974 and the European law of human rights. As managers and employees, not only do we have moral obligations, but legal obligations too. It is the law! But our standards do not stop at running water and clean loos and canteens. Our first set of standards reflect on us and our staff how we would like to be treated ourselves during our long, arduous days of toiling for someone else's company. We would like to be spoken to politely and professionally in a mature, grown-up, adult fashion. We do not want to be chastised for the slightest error or ignored when we have something to say. And so, we all, staff and self, begin building on or rather naturally relying on the hierarchy levels of Maslow's pyramid. But these are not the only set of standards we have to work toward. We also have other sets of standards that need tending to. As with customer service, for us as a manager or employer, we have other customers too. Customer service does not just stop or start with the public. As a manager we have other customers. Staff are our customers and we have covered this in some depth, but also, our upper management and our employers or shareholders and, of course, the great general buying public are our customers too. To service these *other* customers and promote ourselves and our 'brand', we have to instil other standards. These are standards of performance, accuracy, presentation, intelligence, rational thinking, organisational skills and communication. We have standards of behaviour, rules and regulations and standards of pride in what we do and how we go about our daily work life and so on. Although this list is not exhaustive, it simply shows how we operate as managers. This is how we build ourselves a brand. This how we become known to peers and supervisors. This becomes our modus operandi. It is how we apply that rational, sensible thought of moral standards across our business and convey to others how we like to operate. Enforcing good standards comes with time and experience. As managers we learn how to do things, how the company like things done and some go the extra mile to try to do things better and, therefore, set a higher or better standards. (Shiny bicycle lamps!) Eager to please or show high standards of operating, some managers take on too much and fail, therefore allowing standards to fall or slip, causing them stress or anxiety as they attempt to yet again improve. Operating at a high standard comes with practice and is only made easier with time and skill. Object management comes before project management.

Show me, Tell me

When we discuss and debate standards it is most important to remember that we all come from different backgrounds and, therefore, we are likely to have differing standards. This is not a bad thing as the more ideas the better, usually, but when we begin to work as part of a team, clearly we need one outcome or one standard for a particular subject. Also in the interests of fairness we need set standards that allow all team members to aspire to or to achieve and, as managers, when we expect people to deliver to our standard, we can often forget the problem of differing ideas and backgrounds with experience or lack of it playing into this scenario also. A simple cleaning task, presentation job giving personal care or stock moving exercise can deliver itself in many differing individuals' standards. As mangers, we would be expecting a standard that allows us to move on and not get bogged down by details or lengthy repetitive training exercises. To prevent this problem the good practice of 'show me, tell me' should be deployed at every opportunity. This act also shows good leadership skill and proper coaching can prevent unnecessary repeats or revisiting of tasks and standard problems. By showing our people what standards we would like and by telling them what we know and why we do things in such a way, we can develop our people to work at and maintain an agreed acceptable standard. Once rolled out thoroughly and accurately this standard can, in turn, be passed on from individual to individual. Once we are satisfied with the standard we can encourage the spreading of its delivery across the whole team. This can be applied to anything and awarding a task some quality time to show staff why and how we would like something done will prevent poor standards and develop our teams and our success.

Signing off

"What does a good job look like?" Earlier we used an example of simply tidying an office, clearing a stock room or sweeping a warehouse. This is how we use standards, first to begin brand building. This is how customers, visitors, clients and the public see us. This is how the little restaurant on the back road gets seen, initially through its physical standards. These standards convey our message that we wish to engage with the wider world and show that we care and we are open for business. It is also how the paying public perceive the message that we give off. Does the little restaurant on a back lane in a backwater town really care? If they cannot be bothered with their *kerb appeal*, which involves basic housekeeping, cleaning and maintenance routines, perhaps they are not too bothered about their kitchen hygiene, as this too involves basic housekeeping, cleaning and maintenance routines. Here the saying holds true. "You will never get a second chance to make a first impression." My personal quote is: "Good presentation standards are great decision-makers."

If we have standards built on strong morals, we can say a job is not complete until we sign it off. Signing off a job can be physical or metaphorical. Signing off a physical job can involve a simple check to say that we are happy with a set standard or are pleased with an outcome. It can quite literally be a signature on a document. Often a head office set-up will send in national contractors to do repairs, refurbishments or general decorating. I used to be surprised by the number of managers who would sign the contractor's paperwork simply to pacify the contractor. The thought of not signing it and getting the contractor to show them the work and standard of finish never entered their heads. Besides, they were too busy managing and had better things to do. Or so they thought. I would despair at times as less experienced managers would accept sub-standard services. As managers it is, of course, our full responsibility on behalf of our company to check that we and our business are receiving the very best service from that contractor. I have in the past demanded contractors redo their work or clean and tidy up before signing a job card or allowing them off the premises. We would not pay a plasterer or decorator at home if the job was terrible, would we? With a little training these issues can always be easily resolved, but to drive these standards higher can often be much harder.

Inside the building, standards are how the place feels. The ambiance and the atmosphere. The lighting, smells, floors polished or swept, the painting of walls, quality of furniture and so on. If everything looks and feels tatty, it probably is and that will be the perception no matter how much protesting from the owner or proprietor. If the customer genuinely feels that the place is unkempt, this will affect the mood and, therefore, the purchasing frame of mind of that client. Do we have stock on the shelves readily available in a neat manner? In retail it is known as 'facing up'. It is how the product is presented to the customer. Using the manufacturer's efforts to brightly and carefully package the product, we show it face up or face front to the buyer and not face down revealing all the packets' endless disclaimers, ingredients or instructions. Paint pots and adhesive or large tubs of washing powders will have all their handles folded forward ready to be grabbed should the customer go ahead with the purchase, all there, stood to attention, face front, like soldiers on parade, ready to persuade the buyer to go head. 'Sign off' is not only for contractors. Staff too can try shortcuts, so be firm, but polite. Show and tell again until happy with the output. Only when we are happy staff have achieved the required standard should we sign it off. Even if we are managing a supply based department if the stock is neatly displayed and well laid out this will make the task so much easier and efficient. In all cases shelves should be dust free and clean of residues, well labelled or priced to show that the products have constant turn around and humans actually frequent the area.

As with all of 'the Seven Ss' and with all the above, achieving most physical standards does not cost money. Our business need not spend thousands to achieve these goals. Granted, a small investment would normally be required in order to provide quality cleaning equipment, but thereafter it is just a matter of time, effort and a sheer tenacity and a will to succeed in delivering.

Sixty Minutes

Whilst discussing standards we have come across the subject of head office, director or owner visits. One should never dread a VIP visit. I always remember learning that good standards allowed me not to fear visits from my bosses, but to embrace the opportunity to showcase my branch or area and to walk visitors around proudly, quickly identifying areas of change, development and successes. However, stores and branches standards can slip from time to time. The principle here was that I would only ever need an hour to tidy up and present a branch to a director. A quick skirmish around the car park, then the branch itself would normally suffice. Some areas would be 'work in progress', but if we get the standards right elsewhere, we will always be able to hold our head high and show our superiors that we are on the correct path. There are only two visits, expected and unexpected, and if expected, work quickly and diligently with our teams to prepare. Failing to prepare really is preparing to fail. If we ignore the time scale and/or warning and do not invest in preparing for a great visit, we will definitely succeed in not getting one. The 80-20 rule will reinforce this fact. We get 80% out from 20% of our efforts. Before a visit walk the walk and look closely from a customer's perspective. What would the customer see and think as they walk around your business? If the visit is unexpected, being a proactive team manager, we would have developed standards over a period allowing us to present our departments to the unexpected VIP at least with an excusable average standard.

First impressions really do count and here presentation is everything. When preparing for the dreaded visit a good practice is to always work from the front, backwards, but start with the end in mind. Look at your kerb appeal or street view first. Where do you see the start of the customer journey? Start where the customer would start. This could be the entrance or the car park. It is worth mentioning that a VIP visitor does not have specialist eyes, perhaps just a sharper or trained eye with a mind focused on what the customer might see. The truth is, if a VIP visitor can see it, so too can a customer. If the customer does not like what they see, they will vote with their feet and take their customer elsewhere. This is the key point, as the standards we are developing are not for the VIP visit per se, but they are for the benefit of the customer. The VIP is merely commenting on an area worthy of development, to increase sales opportunities perhaps, or an area of concern that may be embarrassing, such as dirty customer toilets, or legally incorrect, such as poor pricing. So the VIP or visitor is like an auditor who will identify areas of concern and expect us as the manager to amend or improve on it. Remember, these rules apply to even a care home, a factory floor or a banking reception area.

Say what we See

I can think of nothing more important each morning than walking our business. By doing this we will firstly set a standard and an example for others to follow and we build our brand. Over a period of time our deputy and teams will accept this as the norm and even action it in our absence. I use to swear by this daily ritual and always used a page a day diary to log down jobs and items that needed addressing. I would frequently encourage deputies and department staff into eventually doing their own daily lists and, therefore, shift responsibility and empower the team (delegating). Continually actioning a daily list of tasks and jobs to be done will gradually reduce, allowing us to focus on more important priorities such as sales or staff development, etc. I would normally work on a list of at least 10 items per day. Ten items was never a struggle. I would always say what I see and write it down. If we maintain this discipline, over a period of time our team will come to expect it and we have then set the standard. Secondly, we will be on a path to success by slowly eradicating problems and developing our presentation and housekeeping standards. Thirdly, this exercise will keep us well informed as to what is happing inside our business and keep us in step with staff and customers alike. If we never use the staff room, we will never really understand what goes on in there. If we refuse to use the customers' parking area and never visit it, how will we know when it needs litter picking or maintenance work? If we never leave our desk or our office, how can we possibly soak up the true atmosphere and reality of the workshop or shop floor? We must not live in an ivory tower. We must actually walk the walk (as opposed to talking the walk) on a regular basis, as this will surely keep our feet firmly on the ground, but more importantly is an absolute strategy that should always be promoted. Failure to exercise this practice is certain commercial suicide.

Using the Seven Ss to improve our standards, we will need to do some homework and research and learn the history. We will need to understand where we currently are. Do we need to understand our competitors? Do they operate to a higher or better standard? Do they operate with better stock availability or better house-keeping standards? Do they have contract cleaners or do their staff do it in-house? Does their customer service exceed customers' expectations? All these questions need investigation, as, for ultimate success, they are all areas where we must excel. So then, visiting our com-petition should not be a strange, unusual or nervous affair. To excel in these areas we must understand our competitors' standards and levels of operation. We can use our SWOT analysis model for this, but first we will need to do a bit of 'mystery shopping' by actually visiting our competitors wherever possible. If we manage a department within a factory, organise a visit to a colleague's department for a coffee and an informal chat and explore how they operate. If we manage a bank branch or section, for instance, go along to a bank of a friend or family member to experience a visit from their perspective. Why not even open up a bank account elsewhere to really experience their true service? I have literally opened trade accounts with competitors solely to establish their standards. I have often taken my partner with me shopping at competitors, posing as genuine shoppers to find out how they really operate and to make true comparisons. Do not think this is strange, as it is a well-known practice and many successful managers use this approach. If it is not part of your firm's culture, I recommend you quietly give it a try. Be discreet and quiet and make some notes. Bring it up for discussion with your manager at an appraisal or a branch visit and explain your reasons and then your findings. You will be surprised by how powerful a tool it can be. Understanding our standards is a great stepping stone to success. Working toward improving our standards can be most rewarding and satisfying, but be honest, good or bad and say what you see.

Spell it out

When pushing through on standards, the practice of a double diary, I found, is one of the easiest management tools we can start with. I would always strongly recommend to ensure that we have two diaries in the business. The first one is our own manager's diary. This should be a proper page-per-day diary and should always be laid out open on the desk for all to see. In it, I would always recommend we aim for a list of 10 tasks ready for the following day using the priority matrix we looked at earlier. Ten things to do is a 'must' and one should keep them individual to us, as these jobs are what we personally wish to achieve for that day. The jobs in this diary will be management jobs. It may seem difficult initially, but with some thought and creativity it should be possible, but do not give oneself impossible or extremely difficult things to do. Keep them realistic and doable in that day. Apply the 80-20 rule and tick them off and highlight them once done. It gives one a great sense of success and achievement and staff will see you achieving and doing. The use of the diary in this way is to help us prioritise our day and help instil standards in how we work and to showcase how we work. Never put personal or sensitive items in this diary; appointments and business tasks are just fine. The correct use of this diary serves several purposes. One, as a diary, obviously; two, a very clear communication tool to our deputies or team. Three, a billboard to show how organised we are with our work and four, it shows our team how we work and how organised and methodical we are and how we achieve and complete tasks ourselves, therefore setting a great example.

The second diary is what I used to call a 'day book' and, as no one can remember everything, this will be used for driving up daily standards with tasks entered in it, but only after walking around our business. As we have said already, we will only get to know our business by walking it and talking to people. Every corridor, restroom and bathroom should be walked and problems detected. I once worked for a firm so committed to this approach that we even had A4 pre-printed 'Things to do' pads. I recommend marking the book clearly so all the team are aware and familiar with it and its purpose. It is important to explain how important this book will be. This book can be left in an office, but ideally it should be somewhere fully accessible to all team players. The culture shift here is to get every member of staff involved and to view the day book on a daily basis. The only role with the 'day book' is to allow any staff member to walk the business and write down what we see, good or bad. If something is wrong and needs fixing, write it in the book. If a new fire exit sign is required ordering, write it in the book. If something needs cleaning, write it in the book. If you have a question about something, write it in the book. If a toilet is broken, write it in the book. Do not worry about aiming for 10 items here, as there will normally be more than 10 tasks requiring correcting, so fill the page. The job will still remain whether you write it in or not, so writing it down there and then shows that you care and are proactive and not procrastinating or being lax with your obligations. On the left-hand side number each task and on the far right put a person's initials against it showing who you would like to do the task. This helps share the burden of tasks evenly, as some staff will avoid tasks and others will do more than their fair share. When done and signed off they should initial the task as complete. As with the desk diary in your office, encourage staff to highlight the entries and sign them off when done (for praise and coaching purposes), but do not allow the entries to be obliterated with markers, as it is most important that we keep both these books as a record of performance (corporate safety cushions) and a reference of when tasks were done and completed for health and safety or trading standards reasons. The book will show we took action on such a date. The point is for your team members to look in the book freely and willingly each morning to see if there is any task or job required of them or their department. We also can leave notes, request small errands and generally show that you wish to communicate with your teams.

Once we have embedded this second diary (day book) behaviour we can delegate this task out to a junior or deputy and use the whole system as a coaching tool to help them develop and learn how to manage things for themselves. Eventually we can apportion smaller sections of departments to give general assistants ownership, responsibility and empowerment. Soon, through this embedded routine, staff will become familiar and comfortable to do their own day books and walk-arounds and do their own jobs lists. Here, our role becomes that of coaching and monitoring to check staff are, in fact, looking at the right things and prioritising tasks correctly. In the main I can confirm it really does work and can free up our mornings immensely. This really is empowerment, so spell it out loud and clear.

Signs

Another standards issue that reflects on managers and has been a bug bear of mine for years is the business of putting up notices in the hope it solves a problem with little management input. Although not exhaustive, there are a few that stand out. "Please wash your pots. Please dispose of your rubbish. Please turn off lights off. Caution, hot water!" I believe the examples here merely push problems to one side and do not deal with the standard directly. If we have no standards in our standards, what sort of managers are we? Simply putting a note out has not improved the temperature of the water to an acceptable level. Here the managers are aware of the problem, but have done nothing about it apart from wasting ink! The underlying problem is a lack of involvement, pride, responsibility and/or ownership. Put simply, poor standards. Why not call the plumber or dial down the thermostat? By swinging the pendulum of coaching, it is better to work with people to embed a culture and to encourage people to clean and tidy up after themselves as they go along. Managers should teach and lead, explaining and showing why it is important to do so. If it is important enough to warrant a note or poster to be erected, surely that issue warrants closer attention and resolution. As managers we should look to remove posters from walls and notes from fridges or sinks. Our work should be to remove these problems by changing attitudes and perceptions. Management should work with teams and apply peer pressure if offenders cannot respect a tidy communal space. Alas, with so many signs and posters erected giving instructions and commands, our staff simply fail to notice the important signage and see it only as decorative wallpaper!

Shelving

Once all posters and notes have been removed and 'remain' removed, the evidence is clear. Success! It shows that management are back in control and, in fact, showing leadership by servicing the needs of all team members and the business. Preventing the need for any more posters is a style of leadership and branding by the manager to maintain a status quo. This style is a reflection of the individual and represents his or her standards of operation. Alas, putting up more shelves in order to resolve untidy areas is not the correct response to the problem. As I moved up through my early management years I became specialised in the restructuring and cleansing of warehouses. The thought process of predecessors was to put in more warehouse racking, which, in turn, gave more shelving. This only exasperated the problems and staff simply put more stock and goods on the shelves in attempts to tidy. This was merely a temporary fire-fighting approach and caused great expense in both equipment and manpower. My approach was to remove (and sell it off for best price) the said racking and, therefore, reduce shelving, forcing personnel to deal with the real issue, which was the problem of too much stock! My approach was to sell it off, ship it out to other branches or, as in a few severe instances, force the stores ordering teams to pallet truck (often tons of it) in and out of the warehouses daily until it was all gone. This approach forced the ordering teams to look at the stock (face the problems) every day and, therefore, deal with the issue daily and focus on accurate ordering. Then as the queue of pallets slowly reduced we would manage and monitor the situation daily with use of the diary 'day book.' Using the day book, this in turn allowed the teams to prioritise and work their way through all of the problem stock until it was gone or at least clear of the warehouse floor. Thereafter, we would use the sequence management tools of monitor, measure, maintain, move and manage. After years of slow decline in warehouse and ordering standards this approach reinvigorated and reinstalled a high standard required in the warehousing and storage sector of the business.

On reflection, we can see our standards come from many sources. We have many established standards that come from within and other standards that we learn or borrow. There are many ways to drive standards and mostly they are cost-efficient. Having high standards comes at little or no cost. To achieve and maintain high standards simply takes time, tenacity and patience. Obviously, there can be certain costs for materials to support, but most of them will come from the people with a little care and inclusion. Persuading people, with a little peer pressure, also makes achieving and the success of standards so much easier. Getting people on board can make a whole difference and success so much more accessible. Consistent high standards are key ingredients for delivering world-class service and completing our branding package.

"Start with the end in mind."

Stephen Covey

Chapter 4
Stock

Stock

Some of us may not sell items. It may be that we work in the care industry or the civil service or accountancy, but if we can find the metaphor for stock within our business it will offer the same outcomes. As shoppers and consumers we are all familiar with scanning products at the checkouts in order to collect and pay for our products. So too have we have all got a little annoyed when the product we have spent hours online looking for, trawling the internet and desperately searching for is 'declared not in stock' and, therefore, will not drop into our virtual checkout 'basket'. It is so annoying and can sometimes feel quite desperate, especially if it was for an imminent anniversary gift for someone such as Mother's Day or Christmas. We have all experienced this, I guess, and then we curse the supplier under our breath and bang the escape key to type in another search engine option to look for another supplier. This occurring problem could be due to a high surge in demand, but more often it is down to poor supply or management replenishment issues.

We may be familiar with scanning our products at the self-serve, but not everyone will be familiar with the system itself, before we reach the tills. This scanning and reading of the product's barcode is known as the EPOS (electronic point of sale) system. The beep that we all hear is just a reassuring signal that the sale has been captured and recorded. The system accepts the product, which is then logged as a sale on the day's ledger and deducted from the businesses stock holding. This deduction information will be stored in the computer system and passed to another part of the process, ready to be replenished and automatically replaced in due course. By now most of us will have been brought up on barcodes. Although these barcodes have reduced in length over time the concept remains the same. Nowadays, with improved technology and smarter systems these barcodes or stock-keeping unit numbers (SKUs) are much shorter, with approximately eight numbers. A barcode or SKU carries all the relevant information required and is unique to that individual product. When I first started out most barcodes were 13 digits long and mostly started with 501. The first three numbers indicated the product's country of origin. The next four digits referred to the manufacturer. After this came the five digits unique to the product, describing what it is, its dimensions, texture, colour and so on. The thirteenth and last number was a computer cross-reference check number to prevent confusion with any similar products. As an example we could take two almost identical cans of cola. They may look almost exactly the same except one is diet or possibly 30ml smaller. White emulsion may be identical but for its finish after its application, satin or matt. Peaches may look identical, but some may be from France and some from Chile and so on. The barcode tells the computer exactly all this information. The computer does not read the numbers, as these are purely for humans to identify and work with. The system reads only the thickness of the black lines to identify the single unit. As discussed earlier, once scanned it will acknowledge the sale and then deduct the product from its total stock holding and then that information is used in the reordering to replenish. Today with self-serve tills in supermarkets being used more and more, even the exact weight of the product is included into the code, which will explain that annoying announcement we all love: "Unidentified product in bagging area!"

So we all know what stock is, right? If we are a retailer, we will no doubt know, but if we are in the service sector it may not be so commonplace, but it could be that our work is in manufacturing. Whatever we call it, one thing that will remain is that whatever we are selling or providing is our stock. If we manage a production area, our stock will be the parts or pieces we and our team need to make up the assembled product to pass on down the line. If we are in catering, our stock will be the ingredients and, therefore, the dish advertised on the menu. Even if we sell leisure activity days, the activities are our stock. If we offer motor racing, quad trekking and hover crafting, archery or clay shooting, these are our products. In finance, we may be responsible for bank and savings accounts. These will be our products that our team may have to sell. We may be running a cleaning company. We may offer specialist deep clean services or night-time cleaning. We may offer floor stripping and polishing. Again, these are our products or stock. An estate agent builds up a portfolio of properties to sell, referring to them as stock.

Whatever the products, if we do not have the right stock or the right mix of stock, we will always be, quite literally, selling ourselves short and missing out on sales opportunities. We may run a small hotel and here we will need the rooms (our stock) and restaurant (placings or covers) always readily available for every sales opportunity, but if every room is available except the honeymoon suite, we will never sell honeymoon suite stayovers. Understanding this stock concept will allow us to project our thoughts and visions to ultimately realising more sales. Once we begin to get a better understanding of our stock we can then begin to manage the issues preventing us from optimising our stock holding.

Stock Market

The phrase stock market is a hangover phrase that was used in its original form long before the arrival of stocks, shares, bonds, dividends and ventures, etc. It meant, literally, the stock (cattle) market where animals were bought and sold as far back as Saxon times. Now, stock is usually a large supply and storage of goods, materials or products and whilst we should not refer to people as stock normally (but to encourage a thought process here and keep it within the context of the book) we can also treat the services done by people as a product or stock. Once we clearly understand our products (or services) we can then begin to understand our stock. Without stock we have nothing to sell. If we provide services, say a driving activity experience or a cleaning service, our stock are our skilled people plus the equipment they use. The driving instructor, the car and the test track are the ingredients of the product. The cleaners and their equipment are the product. If we have these in good supply to meet any sales demand, we have stock. Though we should never look at people as mere commodities, for the purpose of the exercise we often need to combine a skilled person with materials to give us stock. A teacher is a product and without a stock of them the head cannot run a school and so on.

Supply and Demand

Getting product supply right isn't easy, yet it is absolutely critical to sales success. If we are in manufacturing or finance, for example, it can be somewhat easier, as our stock will be dictated by the end products. Unlike manufacturing, inventory management or franchise management where managers already have lots of data and analytical tools to help guide decision-making for optimisation, retailer stock can be more unstable. Getting demand wrong can be painful and an uphill struggle. Getting supply right can be a fine art, but once accomplished to a high standard it can be maintained easier, but again once neglected for even a short length of time can become a painful lesson. Here, it is a good idea to focus our attention away and on other departments and begin to build and improve relationships with the supply chain or purchasing departments in our bid for success. We should learn how the system works and find out where the pitfalls are likely to be. Is the ordering department up to the new challenge since our arrival or promotion? Will it be able to cope with the demand once we release our freshly whipped up sales team? Have we fulfilled all previous orders and have we prioritised already waiting customers? If we start as we mean to go on and think outside the box by walking our business and pushing our nose into other areas and if we seek and search for a better understanding of those areas before committing heavily to being reliant on them, if we can understand their problems and issues, it may explain why the poorer sales and stock issues were there originally. If we look hard to really understand the relevant issues, we can begin to assist our colleagues and peers in making stock flow easier and work to our advantage. We should network and brainstorm to resolve the supply problems and understand the demand issues. The smoothness to deliver to our departments what we need and want is key to our supply and demand success.

As a manager one of our tasks is to develop our stock, stock holding and stock control and then, of course, the supply. Whatever it is we sell, we need to have a good reliable source and flow of stock. That may be pallets of products sitting on a warehouse floor or a shelf, or a mix of materials ready to manufacture or assemble, or a pool of people trained, motivated and ready to work. Whatever our stock, probably the most difficult management task we will face day after day is stock management and the single biggest constant problem will be the accuracy of our stock file. Just when we were so desperate to gain more sales or hit our budget, just when we were about to make the last batch or book the last product out, we realise we do not have what the client wants.

Maybe we don't have the size, the colour, the weight, the right style or the right model. Or possibly it has been stolen, broken or returned, but not registered back in as a 'returned item'. Central distribution centres were supposed to help combat many of these problems by improving the supply. This left the art of managing the demand down to the sales management teams through experience, data, and accurate forecasting and projection.

In some businesses, I have seen staff just too busy to order stock correctly or accurately. They quite literally had too much workload to allow them quality time to order correctly. In one business, the staff were so busy putting away 'too much' stock and trying to find homes for it all that it was too difficult to see what they had ordered initially. These cycles can become perpetual.

Customers hate hunting and exhausting searches for products they want, but later find out they cannot have. This includes hotel rooms, gym memberships, cars, cheap flights, bank accounts, mortgages and insurance policies and even more especially when it has been offered earlier at a special offer deal prices. When the stock is exhausted but the demand keeps coming they can get most irate. Making sure that it is not us or our stock replenishment team at fault will ensure we are clear of blame and will identify the weaknesses in the supply chain. The only trick remaining is to make sure we have done everything possible within our power to cover the loss or shortfall in a smart and professional manner. Over the years I frequently shipped stock across stores and branches (even loading up my own car) to eliminate and best reduce the shortages until the supply chain caught up with the demand of the sales.

Service Levels

With stock comes service levels. Once we have established what our stock or products are (including services provided) we can then focus on our service level (stock levels). We have looked at understanding our stock. Understanding the service level is simply a measure, usually in percentage, of that stock to inform us if we have enough of it, whatever it is we are selling or making. If we are manufacturing, our stock will be raw materials. If we are in banking, are the packages and special accounts all available and not withdrawn? If we are in tourism, are all the activities and visitor attractions offered open and available? If we are a fish and chips shop, do we have enough cod for the day's sales? If we are a shipbuilding yard, do we have enough steel sheets and rivets for today's shift? If we offer 10 different activities and have 10 instructors readily available to deliver all 10 activities, we have a 100% service level and are budgeting for 10 sales. Therefore, should I have one instructor call in sick, immediately my service level would drop as I could not deliver that product. In these people examples we can see that if you do not have a pool of staff or you have the people, but they are not trained properly to deliver that service, we will consequently be low on stock and, therefore, have a lower service level, causing us to struggle to maximise our sales opportunities.

A service level means just that. In sale talk it is the level of service we can offer our clients and the amounts of stock we need to operate on a daily basis. We measure service levels as a percentage. If we advertise for sale one hundred products and we have one of every product readily available all of the time, we have a 100% service level. If we sell one of those products, but cannot replace it, our service level drops automatically to 99% and so on. If replenishment of products is delayed or not possible within the trading day, our service level will gradually drop and drop. This may be our operating business model and replenishment may happen overnight or in a few days. However (depending on the product), research after research shows that a customer will grow impatient and go elsewhere if what they want is consistently unavailable to them. The trick here then, to maximise sales, is to maintain our service level throughout the trading day or trading period. If we have monitored, measured and managed our sales records we will have figures to show historic selling patterns. These records can guide us to developing our service level and to maintain it to an optimum level. The records may show that, on average, every Friday we sell approximately 50 battered cods or three junior savers accounts. The management process now is for us and our teams to understand and be comfortable with ensuring there is enough stock to fulfil those sales or orders. Isolated, this might sound easy, but at times this requirement 24 hours a day, seven days per week, and possibly by hundreds if not thousands of products, can be challenging.

Understanding your service level system is key. Again you can start by walking your business and talking to your teams. What do they know? What can they tell you? You may have bought a business or taken over from someone

PAUL FITZSIMMONS

else. What information could they share? A good set of accounts will not identify how the sales were derived initially and cannot show where the improvements can be made. Also, sometimes smaller companies do not always keep track of every detail. If this is so, we should begin to build our own sales and stock records, finding a way to itemise and categorise sales at the very least A Microsoft XL type programme can help us do this if there is nothing in place. If we work in a modern retail or manufacturing environment, we will undoubtedly have a tailored replenishment system. Even the smallest of filling station garages operate automated EPOS systems nowadays. To maximise sales it would be prudent to initially understand and gain a better understanding of how that system works. If we have a team of people who work this replenishment system for us, it would still be prudent to get to know how the procedures or systems work, as for our part as a manager we will be expected to grow our sales and the easiest way to do that is to get the system working at maximum efficiency for us. If we can manage this, we can begin to grow sales from our very next delivery of stock. We may not have to understand the system fully if we have a team of others to do it for us, but we will need a good working knowledge to help and support our staff if things go wrong, as computer systems often can and do.

Stock Control

The beauty of this computerised system is that it will guide you into avoiding what is known as 'out of stocks' or gaps on shelves in your product range and it will collate and store data and statistics for you. If you do not have a system like this you can still encourage your teams to record individual sales. Most modern cash tills will give you an idea also by allowing itemised sales by department. By department can still be vague, so try to retain your sales copies. Also, spend some time to 'drill down' through sales categories into your subcategories to find repeat or offending problems or gaps.

We have looked at a simple service level example and how selling that one product reduces your service level to 99% and so on. If we take that simple logic idea and multiply it to real-size world sales problems, it is easier to see how things get more difficult. It may be that you have one hundred products, but as a good practice you may stock or hold three or four of everything. If you still only sell one of a product and only sell one per trading day, your service level for that day will remain at 100%, because you still have two items of the same product remaining to service any more sales requests of that product for remainder that day. (Take caution, though, as you will only have three if not two days' worth of sales.) So the real trick here is to understand and interpret your sales data and sales volume. Seek and search. These systems are not forecasting programmes. They are fact-based only systems and can only work off accurate sales data. Once the system has a collection of sales information it can analyse and compute these figures, giving estimates and averages based on previous activity. A good EPOS system will build up average weekly sales records for you and will show you trends and patterns when stock was sold and it can also give you daily reports on your current service levels. For service levels to operate, we mentioned per operating day, but this is only an example of time units based on modern central warehouse retail deliveries. The service level figures will always be operating to your own delivery dates, but, since nearly all businesses operate on a weekly sales forecast, an EPOS data collection of sales will normally be based on a weekly basis. However, as a manager this brings with it another high-intensive area of weekly management.

Today, as computer performances are enhanced and improved, many businesses do not even require human intervention to replenish or maintain their service levels, as products and stock in general will be automatically pre-programmed and reordered from central distribution warehouses. If this is so, a better understanding will still be required and beneficial as a manager, to strengthen any weaknesses in your company's or depot procedures. As a manager involved in the selling or the providing sector of any business, it will probably still need us to improve or manage well these service levels systems.

Stock Reduction

As a manager we will almost always be monitored and measured on stock holding and will inevitably hold a budget of pounds sterling or dollar figures to adhere to. This may often be a percentage of your sales or pro-duction output. Balancing this particular book can be exhausting, especially if you operate a larger retail or manufacturing outlet such as a supermarket or assembly plant. Even with stock teams, a general manager will still have overall responsibility for replenishment and having a good skilful working knowledge of this system can be quite time-consuming. Also inheriting and reducing a large over-budget stock holding business can be a lengthy and time-consuming business. One cannot simply write off stock and dispose of it. There are profit, budget, shrinkage and even tax implications. Here the stock needs to be managed and reduced to a controllable level. Stock reduction exercises are a positive step in the right direction. Cleansing stock rooms, clearing the clutter and casting off slow-moving lines can vastly improve not only our ordering and, therefore, selling performance, but also stock holding and shrinkage results, making us more successful managers. This can be done via small sales promotions, discontinued runs, sale or return, supplier buy backs or rebates, reduced to clear and shipping out to other branches; these are all ways of clearing out stock without causing shrinkage problems. To sustain high-quality service levels we need to ensure a steady flow of the 'right' stock throughout the week. This will be easy if the EPOS system works smoothly and all colleagues process every item correctly and thieves are good enough to at least tell us what they have taken or damaged!

Do we manage our sales system to an optimum service level? If the answer is no, for one, we will not have a 100% service level and two, we will be losing out on sales or vital productivity and missing many unknown opportunities. Managers will always be measured on service level standards and it would be prudent to manage it wisely. Understanding whatever systems we have in place and then deciding if they are adequate enough will help us constantly replenish and meet the demands of our sales from our clients. If we struggle to do this, but are still sales savvy, we may have to manage a large 'stock to order' based system instead, which means constantly promising clients from a future delivery. It is far better to sell immediately rather than to run up a large order base.

The management of this system will vary from business to business or may even include introducing one, but, once understood and shared with staff, it will bear fruit. It will require patience and understanding, but, if we persevere, we will reap its rewards and eventually put to bed stock availability issues and improve sales or production. Rogue products and problematic suppliers will always be part of our daily life and we will possibly struggle to change these issues. However, with a more accurate understanding of stock issues we will be able to identify to line management, suppliers or buyers where the missing or problem issues are, or indeed what new opportunities we have identified. Some businesses nowadays are so proactive to correct these product supply problems that they will outsource and have on standby replacement products to optimise their business service levels and, therefore, support their sales or manufacturing teams.

In the end days of the Focus DIY Ltd chain, before it eventually folded, it desperately tried to improve its stock holding levels to gain improved sales. Every evening store managers were instructed to and would frantically go through their stores scanning every missing product from the shelves and pegs, with a handheld terminal in an attempt to override the ordering system and get stock back into their stores and onto their shelves. Had the drive to restock been managed properly much, much earlier, their 'offer' (supply, stock, sell, service) could have been so much improved.

"Knowledge is power."

Anon

"You never get a second chance to create a first impression."

Mark Twain

Chapter 5
Sales

Sales

People buy from people. This rule is proven over millennia. Sales may be the world's oldest occupation, but a lot has changed since its early days. Sales has evolved from the simple act of swapping a goat for corn, or a pig for rice and later, with the introduction of coinage we moved to bartering methods and then later still, to the emergence of sales methodologies and intelligent tools. There has never been an alternative and in today's modern, 24-hour, commercial and capitalist societies being a sales manager can be one of the toughest areas of management, as it is the sales that drive the progress or success of business and economies and, therefore, that is fundamental to all business development. With sales it can be a real roller coaster of a ride, up one day and down the next. Some businesses can be ruthless in extracting the sales they need and your performance can be as good as yesterday's sales figures. Your sales performance as a manager can make or break you.

This book is not intended to be a sales guide or a tutorial. There are thousands of books out there that do that. The aim of this book is to signpost where sales sits in our scheme of management, to help remind us why we actually go to work and to prompt us to visit our sales on a regular basis. The intention is not to instruct on how to sell. That would require much more studying and skilled experience. Due to its very nature, sales falls sequentially and logically into the Seven Ss and we as managers should visit this subject or department daily, even hourly or at the very least in the morning and then the afternoon, as sales is the very essence of what we do.

Whether it is national health, farming, a charity organisation or human resources, our work in management will always be driven by results and what we do with sales. Even the NHS is driven by results, statistics and spending. Almost everything has a point of sale. Even large charities run on sales targets and it can be make or break for them too. Charities such as St John Ambulance, for example, which you may think relies totally on donations. Well, in part, like all large charities it does, but what it doesn't do is sit around waiting for money to roll in. The charity proactively goes out and, through professional third-party agents, generates itself an income by literally door knocking and selling to the public all the good work it does. These door knocker agents are strictly sales targeted. Oxfam shops and the like have weekly targets and budgets to hit too, to help pay their high street shop rentals. Again this is all driven by commerce and the act of selling. Anyone working in business and commerce will be paid on the back of a sale somewhere down the sales chain and on delivery of these are our sales performance. So we should not think we do not have any sales involvement. Quite the contrary.

Seven Steps to Selling

The oldest paradigms in the discipline of selling history are the seven steps to selling. This is a very powerful method when used by a skilled sales force. As its name suggests, it consists of seven steps and describes a typical sales scenario: One, prospecting – searching for new and potential customers. Two, pre-approach – researching the prospect and collecting relevant information before the actual sale. Three, approach – the first few minutes of the sale and making an impression. Four, presentation – demonstrating a product, listing its features and the benefits. Five, overcoming objections – countering customer objections and removing the sense of hesitancy of the customer. Six, the close – successful completion of a sale, and seven, the follow up – saying thank you and making sure that customer is happy (sometimes with the intent of generating a repeat sale).

How will our personal performance be measured? If we sat down with our boss once a week or every month, on what would our performance be judged? We should ask ourselves how we will be measured. The answer to this question would be by our own personal achievements, our overall sales or the achievement of a team of salespersons whom we manage. As discussed earlier, our sales and, therefore, sales performance can be hampered by a poor service level, customer service, high shrinkage, discounting margins, therefore making it of paramount importance we understand the supply and control of our stock and how it is sold.

Clearly, we are far, far more sophisticated nowadays, but the concept remains and we should remember that a business always requires fresh meat (ideas and sales). When growing and developing our business it is a good strategy to keep in mind the hunting analogy and that sales staff (hunters) are trained to the very highest standards. Getting the staff element right is so important, especially sales staff. Without great sales staff, hitting those targets can be an enormous challenge. This is where it pays to invest well, not just in money, but also in time spent with sales teams, coaching and developing them. Train and retrain and then manage their training and performance constantly for best results.

Nothing Gets in the Way of a Sale

If there is one sales mantra that I absolutely believe in, it is this one. Absolutely nothing, I mean nothing, should get in the way of a sale. There is nothing wrong or illegal with pushing a sale as long as the sale is legal and the contract can be fulfilled, then morally and legally all is good. However, it can be amazing how many problems can be created that actually prevent a sale. Protocols, policies, bad practices and even poor sales people not suited to the role can become a problem. Pallets of stock, cluttered aisles, poorly parked trolleys and poor displays can all cause blockages, not to mention poor stock availability. All these can hamper impulse purchasing and cause buyers to lose interest if their wants become difficult to obtain. Therefore, as mangers part of our role is to remove any barriers that may prevent the closing of a sale or a deal. As mentioned, these barriers could be physical, habitual or procedural or even emotional since many purchases are made on a whim or a want rather than a pragmatic need.

Selling Points

When in sales we will come across selling points. KSPs and USPs. These are our 'key selling points' and our 'unique selling points' and we should be mindful not to confuse the two. Some companies and firms see them as the same or just confuse them, but I do believe them to be quite different. All companies have key selling points. When comparing two like for like businesses, we see that these are the main activities. Key selling points tend to evolve from that business's growth and become its natural strengths focusing on products, services or techniques that work and sell well. These are key selling points. In other words what the company does to keep them in the game. A unique selling point on the other hand is exactly that. Something absolutely unique that would be difficult to replicate or offer, or simply something that your competitors just aren't doing currently. A unique selling point is what financial backers and investors look for in new firms to help give guarantees for stronger returns on their investments. A USP could be a product, a satisfaction guarantee, a service or a price. Whatever it is, it has to be something that no one else is offering.

A filling station may say, sell diesel, petrol, LPG paraffin and gas. These products (our stock) are our key selling points, as they are key to our business. We may also sell newspapers and flowers, but these are not our key products to operate as a filling station. Clearly a filling station provides products to keep a vehicle on the road, so selling wiper blades and batteries might also be our key selling point. Another key selling point would be an offer or a product or price set at a special level or amount to allow us to engage in being active in the marketplace, but they are not unique. However, the more of these products, the stronger the KSP offer. The filling station down the road could quite easily replicate our offer at any time. In contrast the filling station example could be almost exactly the same as the opposition, but the only one in town to be open 24 hours. This would obviously be the unique selling point. We may sell patent or copyright-protected products. This would be our USP.

As an area manger once for a large tile retailer my hands were tied with budgets and the purchasing was all done at head office. To beat my competitors I trialled an offer of a free, no obligation home visit, with a measure and consultation service, where my mangers went to the clients' property armed with swatches and brochures, then with professional local tilers signed up to do the work, we developed this to offer a fitting service also. Therefore, we evolved the offer to a complete bespoke service. This became our USP. Are you doing something that the competition is not? If so have you capitalised and cashed in on it? If you do not have a USP, find one. If purchasing and price is out of your remit, create one like I did. Make customer care, satisfaction guarantee or a buy back returns policy your USP. Read your company's mission statement. You may be able to develop that further to gain the edge. As part of your SWOT analysis, survey your customers and find out what they would like.

So we can now see a unique selling point defines our company's unique position in the marketplace, getting us to the heart of our business: the value we offer and the problem we solve. A strong USP clearly articulates a specific benefit. One that competitors don't offer and that makes us stand out. If all the products appear to be the same, our prospective customers won't know which one is right for them. Being clear about our unique selling proposition helps customers differentiate between the varieties of choices available to them. It is a crucial part of effective selling, especially online where consumers have so many options. A USP can also serve an important role internally, as it forces us to consider our company's mission and its very reason for being. As business managers, we need to consider and communicate who our business is for, what drives us to offer the services we offer and how we want to make a unique impact. Our USP is our key differentiator and the reason our customer will buy from us.

Zappos is an online shoe store and there is nothing especially unique about selling shoes online. However, their selling point is unique: free returns. There is no penalty whatsoever to returning a pair of shoes you don't want, a major convenience to customers. Toms Shoes is a shoe manufacturer. Again, there is nothing especially unique about that, but Toms Shoes' unique selling point is that for every pair of shoes a customer purchases, the company donates a pair to a child in need. Toms Shoes helps put shoes on needy children's feet; this is their unique selling point.

USPs are by their nature unique to each business, but roughly fall into three QPS major categories. Quality – superior materials or ingredients, superior craftsmanship, proprietary manufacturing methods and one of a kind. Price – the lowest price guaranteed, price matching, free shipping, bulk discounts and special offers. Service – 24-hour customer service, free returns, satisfaction guarantees and customer support line. For established companies, the USP can eventually become synonymous with their brand, to when the company's name is automatically associated with the unique value proposition that the brand offers.

Stack 'em High and Sell 'em Cheap

For a quick win, this is always a positive, low-cost way to gain sales. If it is top line sales figures you need in a hurry, this approach is a winner. Finding products that are relatively cheap, usually small and easy to carry and have a generic use will generally move quickly. If we take a look at the explosion the UK has experienced in the super-bargain Poundland-type shops, we can see that this method works. Having a popular product range of everyday items that everyone can use and need, with readily available stock, to pick up and take away easily is a philosophy that has proven to be a winner. Once we have identified a product or group we can employ our stock management skills to supply the demand. Stacking products high serves several purposes. One to make a focal point and promotional attraction and two, to show we have plenty of stock of this product readily available, and three it suggests 'in vogue' and, therefore, creates a want to buy, as everyone else is doing it. This approach can be used on services too. Banking, insurance or school sales teams can verbally create the same offer with call to arms slogans such as 'hurry whilst offer (funding or placements) lasts'. Usually a product or service of this nature will have a low profit margin, so the purpose of running the promo in the first instance is to make the profit with the mass selling of stacking 'em high and to drive footfall or gain greater exposure.

Speculate to Accumulate

Once we have decided to use the 'stack 'em high' approach it pays well to research what might move quickly without too much risk of being bogged down in dodgy stock. You may have access to funding to sell more services or have the freedom to order more items. Here seasonal or historical information, statistics or data will assist us in making a good choice. One example I always use is, once, as a store manager, during an above-average British summer I began by overriding the ordering system and ordered in cheap electric fans from China by the pallet load. At first two large pallets to test the theory, then we would order three, four and five pallets at a time. As the pallet of fans arrived we would locate them at the checkout area and they would fly (pardon the pun). We were ordering the next pallet and the next vigorously until other stores cottoned on and the supply became stretched. At the end of the summer my branch had sold the most fans and generated a tidy profit to boot. After the boom, with only one pallet of fans left in the building, the summer ended and we slowly drip fed the remainder fans out of the business with reductions and promo offers to deplete the range and save on precious warehouse space for the autumn. I had speculated to accumulate based on a safe gamble with a low risk return.

Sales Add-ons

Add-on sales can have a big impact on sales and profits. Using this technique not only boosts profits, but can also be seen as giving great service. Selling the main product and then suggesting the need of the add-on products is a most logical progressive step to take. It would be foolish to make and sell a bolt, but not the nut. Or the appliance without a plug, a garden strimmer with its nylon line, a pressure washer without detergents, a table lamp without a bulb and so on. These are our add-ons, the products that support or complement the main purchase. With the boom of mobile cell phones, adaptors, chargers, charging cables and covers, etc. are a prime example of add-on sales. Some staff feel it to be rude, pushy or offensive, but they can be trained to sell these lines. Placing these products strategically around the business can often help provoke thought and invoke a purchase. After clearing some mental hurdles, teams can learn that if you sell someone a battery operated wall clock, it is perfectly reasonable and moral to sell them some batteries also.

Sales Pick-up Lines

As with add-on sales, pick-up lines help boost profits. They are not add-on products and often have no asso-ciation with the main purchase. These sales are simply nice to haves or perceived as must haves or small treats. Again these line or items can be strategically placed around the business to enhance sales from passing traffic. Chocolate or cereal bars for people on the go will always sell at the checkout by encouraging this as an impulse buy.

Sales Floor and Space

If, as we discussed previously, we have brought standards into the equation we should, by now have a clear and safe 'shoppable' sales floor with nothing to get in the way of our sales, be it a car showroom, an office or a corner shop. Our standards, which we said would, over time, become habit and embedded into the business ethos, will ensure clear access to the whole sales experience. Creating ambiance or a positive atmosphere in your sales area or department is crucial to increasing sales. The sales floor or area should be a free and safe buying environment and part of our management role should be a mission to fulfil this objective. Every business unit costs someone something, somewhere. Every building has rent, mortgages or just good old council and business taxes. Therefore, every one of our shop floor tiles or square feet is worth x pounds or dollars per tile, per hour. To increase sales to offset this, wire baskets called 'dump bins' were introduced and we see them placed all over, in the aisles, to hold cheap pick-up lines and generate more 'stack 'em high' quick sales. It does not have to be retail. The IT giants of Google and Facebook and many large websites do this nowadays almost too well, with every inch of viewing screen space flagged by a dropdown, a pop-up, a swipe left or a strap line advertisement offering gimmicks, ads and vouchers when we spend or subscribe and thus inadvertently pass on all our shopping habits.

In the late '80s, many retailers began to grow their market share by opening more stores. Here they simply used the space of the UK to the maximum. However, that strategy later backfired in the following years when sales didn't grow year-on-year. Back in the '90s, my degree thesis work pointed out that large out-of-town stores (including my own company) could not just keep opening new units on retail parks at the end of dual carriageways. Eventually saturation point would be reached and, with no real space left, alternative ways of increasing sales would need to be found. In their defence, they shifted strategy to just simply outnumbering the competition and the game of attrition ensued. Today, space is found on the internet and, as retailers slim down their brick and mortar footprints, they are investing more wisely in e-commerce and employee training. Even shipbuilding companies do not need the sheer space of vast buildings and sheds as more and more is done on computers. Walmart, for example, raised eyebrows when it invested billions in strengthening its e-commerce presence, raising employee wages and improving employee training. Those investments paid off. Walmart is now countering Amazon on multiple fronts. Analysts are praising its cleaner and more organised stores, and shoppers are finally returning. Smart moves like these might make the next year a turnaround year for some retailers. As Bae bought up all the many independent shipbuilders, they realise now that factory work has to be shared across the country and ships are built in segments around the UK.

Seasonal Adjustment

If you are struggling for sales inspiration, stop and search and tune in to the seasons. What do you do? What do you sell? What is the trend? Can you tie into what every customer feels and experiences? The weather and seasons affects us all as consumers, whether we like it or not. We cannot opt out. With the change in climate and weather, so to do our needs change. Parasols, umbrellas, de-icer. It is the same with savings accounts, investments and production. Obviously we all know that the supermarkets are the experts here and are very adept, even into sub-seasonal events such as Valentine's, Easter, Mother's Day, summer holiday vacations and Halloween. Look toward the supermarket approach to learn how they do it. They are past masters and so good that they invent things to suit their own sales objectives and agendas. Who would have thought 10 years ago we would all be drinking fresh water from bought bottles or there would be Valentine's cards for mums or prom dresses for eight-year-olds? If it's sales inspiration you need, look in your local supermarket! Even if you're a health and safety or engineering business you can still create a link and theme to the seasons.

Another seasonal sales driver can be good, thoughtful and well-constructed displays. Even with the smallest amounts of space one can be creative and have a go at a display that should inspire customers and encourage a purchase. This can be from as little as a table-sized trade stall with leaflets to a huge winter wonderland exhibition. Whatever you think will work best for you given the resources. The key here is in the design. Think it through first and plan it out. Use your teams and get buy in. Brainstorm with your people and look at team talent and innovation for quick wins. Obviously keep the display relevant and make it as professional as it can be. It should have a good lasting image, so use colour, textures and vibrant current products to help stimulate the consumer's mind. Allow for a 'touchy feely' experiences so a prospective buyer can see what they could have. I so often came across mountains of stacked plain, boring, brown boxes that do little to inspire and definitely to not urge wallets out of pockets.

Displays alone do not sell. They are supposed to evoke a thought process and create desire. The needs and wants will then be weighed up by the consumer until your sales teams can interact. Another clear way to gain sales from displays is to have the stock readily available and stock adjacent to the display product. If done correctly a good display can encourage a volume of sales, but to really maximise sales and be absolutely certain, we can lay out the stock relevant to that displayed in an orderly fashion, allowing easy access so the consumer can simply help themselves. Manufacturers go to great expense to create colourful and inviting packaging, but nothing beats looking at the real thing and the best display is the real thing supported by the enticing packaging. However, little plain brown or white shipment boxes will do little to shift high volumes, so be sure to open them up and show off good examples and do not leave a stockpile of shipment boxes looking like a barricade.

Signposts and Switch-offs

I visit many, many businesses of all types and sizes. I meet owners and managers alike and it never ceases to amaze me when they cannot see the problems I do, especially on my first visits to their premises. Over the years I have learnt the mantra 'never assume the obvious and always expect the unexpected' as my first rule here. Sometimes getting to a business can seem a near impossible task. Firstly, finding their websites and contact numbers. Some business are so busy being busy that they lose sight of what is important like the basics. Getting the webpage right and guiding potential customers to your store or premises is absolutely critical, even if you are in the manufacturing game. A visiting wholesaler or buyer looking for new products will expect the same standards of clarity and presentation as a retail customer would. Looking for premises and signage, or directional arrows, reading boards and named streets can be made difficult if no effort is made to make it clear. Banners can be used as can posters and sandwich boards. All make the journey more accessible.

Left to our own devices, purchasing can be an easy and quick turn-off for many people and an enthusiastic and excited buying feeling can easily slip away when people are made to work hard before they even get to see the products. Making sure we signpost the whole route and journey will keep the potential customer relaxed and in the buying mood. Ensuring car parks are clean and accessible is another bug-bear for many. If one was to study the psychology of purchasing power and/or the skill of selling and review all the techniques that go into the sale from salesman and from the purchaser, one would know that the access and presentation of the premises along with sales floor should be squeaky clean, polished, free from debris and obstructions. To this day I still find it amazing that customers are allowed to climb over boxes and step over pallets and pallet trucks to get to where they want to be. We talked at length earlier in this book about endorphins and the chemicals that make us feel good and happy. These same chemicals help us purchase items and make us feel rewarded too. Purchase switch-offs can be even smaller than the examples given. Take the stereotypical uninterested, long-suffering husband scenario, being dragged around furniture shops by his wife. She really is in purchase mode, but as usual he is not and the wife knows she needs his financial approval to make the purchase. The slightest thing to switch him off (even lack of signposting) can send them both home empty-handed to watch the football on TV. Items inaccessible or unavailable, aisles blocked off, pallets to be climbed over, displays shoddy and poor. Food served cold, services delivered late or items damaged, lack of interested staff and even missing prices. The husband will look for any way out and won't hesitate to pull your establishment to pieces in order to get to see the match! We are not all grumpy hubbies, however. Some of us just expect basic standards and items to be well merchandised and priced. If we struggle to provide proactive staff to sell, at least we should provide clean accessible display models with plain, clear pricing and plenty of stock. The sales floor environment is so important, as this is where most of us will earn our living and close the sale. I use the term 'sales floor' generically. It doesn't have to be a shop. It could be an office, reception area or workshop. We could be selling ideas or policy, but the concept is the same. It could be a theme park or a restaurant. A play area or a train or a bus. People will and do vote with their feet. It takes tens of years, thousands of pounds and hundreds of thousands of hours to establish a brick and mortar business, so we shouldn't encourage people away to go shop online!

Surveys

As a younger branch manager and without the technology at the time, I once attempted to log the customer flow through my branch using a simple five-bar gate process. We could then look at the number of sales transactions and compare differences. By encouraging my teams to manually record 'footfall' by the hour we could manage team rotas and sales, transparently and inarguably, therefore, allowing us to gear up and down for sales peaks and troughs. This also helped to explain to peers and line managers where and why sales were poor as well as great. This had a dramatic effect on confidence and our ability to sell with conviction. We could also confidently tell bosses why and where things were going wrong and why we were not getting the sales. Armed with clear factual statistics, this allowed me to delegate up and get head office, marketing and directors alike to do a bit of self-critical analysis for themselves.

Once we realise we have a captive audience we can implement short surveys and ask customers outright what they are looking for, what they expect and how we could improve. Once we get over the stigma of being told how terrible we are, we can begin to record survey answers and build up some analysis to help us improve. Here we can implement sequential management using all the Ms: monitor, measure, manage, maintain and mature it (develop area further). I even felt empowered myself and would often walk my stores asking customers how they were finding their experience and had they seen any changes. Obviously I was keen to know what the customer thought and how we could improve on things. These surveys, formal and informal, became mainstream and were worth their weight in gold. I would recommend all managers to get involved in these activities and encourage research at this level. Even if your management role does not involve direct sales I would still urge you to get involved in similar activities. If you are into human resource or production management, for example, then the surveys can still give great feedback. They could show how management could improve staff relationships or help you find how to improve staff performance or develop training. Whatever the department or category, surveys will deliver great results.

Sales Staff or General Assistants?

Many managers by nature of promotion and/or company moves inherit their staff. This presents obvious challenges and especially in retail where many staff are not sales people. They were probably not hired as sales staff, but as general assistants with only a limited amount of sales skills or knowledge. To combat this problem in one large national firm, to boost customer service, I worked with mangers in encouraging all general shop floor assistants to become sales staff, get involved more in the customers' buying process and not just point to the aisle, but to take the customer to the products and then engage. We created some fun around it as an experiment, but in reality it was still a bid to drive sales and service. In those days the checkout tills could not record who had sold what, but through a stop and search exercise I found that staff could ask the checkout operator for a copy of the receipt and write their initials on the slip, thus proving who had made the sale. Collating the tickets, the member of staff with best sales that week got a prize. It was a huge culture change for many, as they were not hired as sales people, but some exceeded and relished the competition and the thrill of a sale. Making the day more fun and with a small amount of excitement, they were free, not just to replenish stock, but to have a go, for the good of the business and for themselves. It was empowerment and autonomy and it was working. We soon built on the success and the better salespersons were given targets and challenges and, of course, prizes. Prizes were not expensive and often were early finishes, late starts or half a day off with pay. The staff really embraced the scheme and the atmosphere in the stores changed.

Sales KPIs

Key performance indicators can be anything you the manager or the company wish them to be. In the sales arena it will normally be something with priority that the staff identify with. This will normally be a range of products that are highlighted. The company will normally select certain stock items and expect these lines to be pushed as a priority or with some preference over other products based on product association or as an add-on. These items can be changed quickly as and when required. Banks can push through special savings accounts; hairdressers may push on perms and colours. A fun park may promote family day packages and a burger bar, a range of spicy products. The main purpose of KPIs is to drive sales and, therefore, profits. However, KPIs can hold staff to account by reflecting individual performance, which then allows managers to monitor sales performance. Daily, weekly, even hourly KPI reports can be generated. I know of one firm where staff would be performance manged down to the very last bottle or last tub. I remember managers holding one-to-one weekly sales meetings in order to instigate sales performance improvement plans to increase the sale of these KPIs. One firm I know of was so fanatically obsessed with their KPIs that they would run hourly reports by individual staff name. KPIs can also be tasks, actions or services implemented in a care home or a school. Put simply, something the firm wishes more of. The theory and philosophy of KPIs does work. If our position as manager involves selling something, as most management roles do, KPIs sales do have their place and can work, but like everything else we have dis-cussed, they too need to be managed!

Point of Sale (POS)

The phrase point of sale came from a combination of price tickets and labels and a UK retail law known as the Sale of Goods Act 1979 (now incorporated under a broader umbrella of the Consumer Rights Act 2015). In UK law, a trader of any sort (engineering, travel, retail or even services in a catalogue) must price a product to make their 'offer to treat' clear to the consumer. A product or service on display (and, therefore, for sale) without a price is technically not on offer. Once the cus-tomer has purchased a product (obviously at some sort of cash desk, reception, till, cash register or checkout or received a receipt, etc.) they have gone beyond the 'point of sale' and, therefore, certain laws on refunds, for example, would now apply. The term became less used, but was embraced by computer suppliers like IBM and EPSON in the bar-coding system such as EPOS (electronic point of sale) and EFTPOS (electronic funds transfer at point of sale). Nowadays it is used even more generically by printing companies who refer to their ticketing, promotional and poster materials as POS.

Now that we understand what POS is and its impor-tance, for the absolute minimum of financial costs point of sale can be used in almost any form to attract and promote sales. We can use POS in conjunction with displays or campaigns to help increase our sales and promote our offers. I say from the absolute minimum cost, because just simply printing a poster on A4 paper becomes POS. A handwritten message on day-glow coloured star-shaped card is POS. Used properly, these cards and messages can partly fulfil a salesperson role, or shout out messages instead of a tannoy announcement. Its most popular use by far is still to price a product on offer. Stationers sell bags of day-glow, star-shaped and oblong coloured card for this very purpose. So whether you are a charity shop or high turnover business, POS can still play a very cost-effective, active role in sales. Many firms use banners and they too are a fantastic cheap way of promoting your trade.

Sell Benefits, not Features

It is not the intention to make this chapter a training manual on sales or salesmanship. There are plenty of bigger and better books out there available for that, but when discussing sales through the use of the Seven Ss, we do acknowledge that in part it must come from educating and coaching the staff we have to help us achieve our successes. Most of us will inherit our staff and teams; if not, we will recruit the best we can from the supply pool we are given. To that end, an important factor that I found invaluable was to get my teams to understand benefits and features. Once this concept is overcome, barriers really do begin to fall within sales teams.

A feature is not a benefit and vice versa. They are totally separate, but once the difference is understood we can quickly become better salespeople as the feature will easily help sell the benefit for us. A good way to remember the rule is that the feature literally does feature in the product. The feature comes first. The benefit comes after. F for first. The feature is a tangible manufactured piece of equipment built into the design or mechanics of a product and a good analogy of this is seen in motor cars. The feature will be four wheels instead of three. The benefit will be that the car will not tip or roll over when negotiating a fast bend. The feature may be a four door hatch over a three door. Clearly the benefit will be easier access to the rear seats with a four-door configuration. A printer feature may be a new improved ink cartridge rather than older conventional models. The benefit may be more printed pages compared to the older model. The feature of a newer, bigger plane is that it is longer. The benefit will be the same number of seats, but with more leg room. And so the list goes on. Features give us benefits. If you can teach your staff this and combine it with add-on sales they will find selling so much easier that it may feel more logical and natural; therefore, creating a win-win situation.

Social Media

Through the invention and development of digital communication, this is truly an area that should be quickly harnessed and mastered for sales. With the huge growth in the use of social media it would be remiss not discuss this, possibly the most powerful, the most cost-effective and the most widely used platforms for marketing any business. It is probably the easiest way to promote and advertise, with very little cost, as the channels open to a user are simply login and 'create an account'. Access to Facebook, Snapchat, Twitter, YouTube and the like are so easy. Since many younger people have been brought up with these now household and branded platforms, they provide easy use and are simple to launch. The lines between media-sharing networks and social networks are becoming ever more blurred these days as social relationship networks like Facebook and Twitter add live and streamed video, augmented reality and other multimedia services to their platforms. However, what distinguishes media-sharing networks is that the sharing of media is their defining and primary purpose, or so it was when first established, but now users can even generate revenue from carefully crafted promotional activity.

SEO

Websites and digital marketing, media-sharing networks and platforms give people, the users and company brands, a virtual place to find and, of course, share media online, including photos, old video and even real-time live video streaming. While the majority of posts on relationships networks contain simple text, business should use a website alongside social media as their main shop window. So much more information and detail can be placed here and today websites can be interactive and used to great effect and able to promote more empathy than a Snapchat slogan. Due to internet algorithms positioning websites in a hierarchy order, websites will be placed in viewing pecking order on screen. It is prudent then to know how you will push your website higher up the pecking order. To do this we can employ the services of a search engine optimiser (SEO). These people will literally rework or reconfigure how the likes of Google sees your pages and working with that information plus several other internet tricks they can quickly push you up the viewing list, but, more importantly, keep you there week on week.

Sales Loyalty Ladder

We have mentioned many times now about building oneself into a brand and being known for something we stand by. The biggest success stories have built themselves into a brand. Any household name is by definition a brand. That could be a product, a company, a manufacturer or indeed, as we have discussed, a person or even a nation. The Germans have built themselves a brand based on consistent sound, reliable, quality engineering and manufacturing. Land Rover ensured consistently that their vehicles outperformed others in off-road scenarios (even if their build quality was not superior).

Dyson consistently proved more suction with its unique bagless fan system.

Once we have established a brand we can explore who and where our customers are. Have they bought from or used us before? Are they a customer or a client? Do they promote or advocate for us? Do they consciously act as repeat buyers and are they brand insistent? Many Land Rover advocates will insist on using a Land Rover badged brolly. Audi lovers will wish to wear an Audi jacket over a plain one. These people are at the top of our loyalty ladder and insist on nothing less. But we need to know and understand this and then work with them when they are in purchasing moods. Some clients may never have used us before, so we then need to work just as hard to make them loyal, to make them brand insistent. How many stories have we heard of a person leaving one business, but taking all their clients with them? Vets, doctors and architects are well known for this. How many people buy from your branch because you are there running the operation? How many would follow if you moved across town to another firm? Once you have people on the loyalty ladder we must keep them on it. If you research how the loyalty ladder works you will find that people are very willing to trial and experiment with new people, but to maintain them over long periods to advocacy is a different challenge.

Sales Journey

Getting things right to find those extra sales is critical and, if we learn to use the Seven Ss to help us achieve this, I believe we are on our road to success. Using our newfound tools the Seven Ss can help deliver us onto a path of improved sales. Some will say that sales are everything as sales pays for everything else and make everything turn, oiling the cogs of commerce. This is quite true, but to optimise our sales and have faith that we are getting everything right we should use our newfound tools in conjunction with the customer sales journey.

Once we understand the customer journey we can combine our new skills with all the resources at our disposal to absolutely maximise our operation, safe in the knowledge that we are taking every possible step to be proactive with the main goal of increased sales in our sights. To see the big picture we can ask ourselves where the customer journey starts. I ask people this question often and seldom get the correct answer. Some say the showroom or the sales office; others say at the cash desk or with a salesman. It is none of these, as the journey for the customer begins as a piece of information in their home or at their workplace through the radio, a TV or newspaper ad. It starts as word of mouth as a comment or a recommendation in their canteen or on the bus home. It can be a random email, a leaflet, a business card in a shop window or a telephone call in the evening. However it comes, if the customer wishes to engage with that information, the journey can commence.

From this initial piece of information (the introduction) will come a line of enquiry and with it a certain level of expectation depending on how the information was delivered. Have we noticed, for example, how airlines and holiday firms present themselves so wonderfully and beautifully in this vein? Here the die is cast and now all involved will have to live up to that expectation. But even then we may not realise that the journey has begun. The prospective client now begins to research, perhaps with a visit to that holiday firm's webpage. In corporate worlds that webpage will usually mirror or complement the TV ad, so the expectation level will remain high. Pleased with their research, the next part of the journey may be a telephone call to the nearest branch. With a professional and hassle-free phone call and with beautiful TV and website images in their thoughts, the journey continues with an invite and a trip to the nearest branch. Now here comes the tough part. Gone are the actors and beautiful handpicked models and carefully scripted conversations. Now we have to deal with real, live everyday people, namely ourselves and our staff, and our standards. Can we live up to those glossy TV expectations? Are we good enough managers and professional salespeople to continue that level of expectation of the journey?

This is where we and our Seven Ss swing into action and this is where all our work on self, staff, standards, coaching, development, training, listening, brainstorming, Maslow's laws and stock comes to fruition. Here is where the expectations will hold or fall. Here is where the buck stops and we make our own success.

"Management is doing things right. Leadership is doing right things."

Peter Drucker, management consultant and author

Chapter 6
Shrinkage

Shrinkage

They say that we are keen to look after the 'front door', but forget the back door. The 'front' is where tills or sales areas are and where we see the customer and, therefore, too the sales opportunities, but it is possible we get too wrapped up in this area with the sheer commercial need to constantly drive at sales and hit our targets and exceed our budgets. It is very easy to neglect the 'back door' where the profits can slowly dribble away and ultimately lose the business thousands. In modern-day management, part of our performance record will inevitably involve a track record of our personal performance in managing shrinkage to within the company's required budget and targets. In short, understanding shrinkage is just as important as understanding our sales, services or production targets. If we are new to shrinkage, it would be prudent to study this subject closely, as it can make or break a manager's overall annual performance!

The word shrinkage is a commercial term for a financial sum that has been lost. It is usually expressed as a percentage and it usually expresses a loss, although we can have positive shrinkage also. It is a mathematical sum, where sales figures constantly clash with stock or service figures to provide an end result figure. Here, the subjects require the strictest adhesion of the company sales and stock rules with solid management and balancing for a positive result. Stock or services provided figures, subtracted from sales, should result in a firm and positive cash figure as a percentage. If there is a difference in that figure, usually less, this is the shrinkage. Shrinkage is a word used for an unforeseen commercial or financial loss. It is also known as inventory shrinkage or profit erosion and was originally thought to be just the loss of stock or products between the supplier or manufacturer and the point of sale. The term shrink relates to the amount of profit margin any company could lose from the loss of that product or service. Every time a product was lost (or service wasted) instead of sold, it would shrink the amount of overall cash profit margin the company was supposed to generate. In later years shrinkage became more technically detailed and better understood, which, in turn, gave managers a better understanding of what control they had over their business, whilst in charge in their role. The Business Dictionary declares it to be the 'difference between book-inventory and physical-inventory due to counting or recording errors, or resulting from pilferage, spillage, theft etc. or an allowance made for reduction in the takings of a business due to wastage or theft'. Another type is 'call centre shrinkage'. A measure of how much time is lost in the call centre due to things like vacation, breaks, lunch, holidays, sick time and training, etc. Shrinkage is normally the slow and stealthy stealing away of money, products, service or time and is difficult to see until a stocktake or stock count is done to measure it or monitor it.

Traditionally, especially in retail and sales, after our business has had a stocktake, a calculation is applied to the business's overall current stock figure, which shows a gap, expressed as a percentage of overall stock versus sales. This figure shows the gap between our actual profit and the profit that we should have generated or the cost of the stock we should be holding. This gap is the shrinkage, as in the shrinkage of our profits. Not unique to retail, every business will experience shrinkage and it will occur for many reasons and can be identified by experts under three different main headings. Stock shrinkage involves product theft, damages, markdowns, inaccurate discounting and price errors. Cost shrinkage involves a general waste in resources, overtime, utilities, gas, electric, rent, equipment and what they call 'paper shrink', which occurs through incorrect accounting, inaccurate counting, administrative issues and poor booking-in and sales registering, all caused by human error. Shrinkage can normally vary between approximately 0.5% and 2% and, dependant on turnover, can be thousands and thousands. However it happens, it is still shrinkage

Slimming Effect

No one loses weight in a day and no one really goes bald in a few weeks and a large mound of sand blowing in the wind will not disappear overnight. As with all these examples, on any one day the effects are difficult to detect. The clear truth with these scenarios is that we lose a very small amount, very gradually over a long period of time. With a slimming plan, we plan to shed a few ounces or pounds gradually over a longer period of time. It is no use weighing ourselves every few hours when the weight loss plan is scheduled over several months. Similarly, we do not go bald overnight, nor is all the sand blown clear immediately. It takes weeks, a few sand grains blown away in the wind here and there with the smallest of gusts. Without monitoring and managing over a reasonable period of time, we cannot measure and realise that things have changed. Perhaps we stop one day and take a cold hard look at ourselves or a partner who has been on that diet. It is only now that we can physically see something is clearly different. We or they have, clearly, visibly and noticeably lost some weight. We might not be able to see exactly where the weight has been lost, but we can see a visible difference. Shrinkage is the commercial slimming effect. This is where stocktakes come in to play. A stocktake is exactly that, taking stock of. It is basically a slimmer's weigh in and will tell us how much weight we may have lost or sometimes gained. It is where months of management control is measured. Like the diet analogy, what stock have we left after all our sales have been taken into account?

Although often convoluted and over complicated by auditors and analysts, shrinkage is very easy to understand and can easily be reduced with common sense and some well-exercised basic management skills. It can take discipline, of course, to check the pile of sand every day or maintain the diet to the letter even though other forces and priorities can seem to constantly pull you away. We can take a brief look at a few scenarios to help explain a little more. If a book has a cost value of five pounds and a mark-up of five pounds, we very obviously have a sale price of 10 pounds. But, if sold at a discounted price of seven pounds, the shrinkage or erosion is mathematically three pounds or 30%. Using this example, we can examine various ways of acquiring shrinkage across a business. If the book publisher sent 1,000 of the same book on a pallet, but with water damage from a warehouse, and we accept that delivery as okay, as a bookseller we will be forced to sell those books at a loss, as no one would want to pay the full price. Or if someone was giving away the books without permission, this would be shrinkage through stock loss. Another form of shrinkage (as seen) may be that your sales team are not quite so good at selling and feel the need to discount the book to a lower price. All quite innocent, but, if, as a bookseller, your job was to sell hundreds of thousands of books per year, each book might be an ounce of weight or a hair or a grain of sand blowing in the wind. The other downside is that you are not receiving the full return on your sales efforts and are now working harder to sell more, but not monitoring and measuring the effects of the diet. Another scenario is possibly staff, in an effort to work quicker and be more productive and, therefore, not focused on the importance of selling pristine quality and condition of the book and throw them from pallet to trolley, to store-room to shelf, inevitably damaging them en route. Again the books cannot be sent back, as the publisher has not damaged them. They now become seconds and again cannot be sold at the full price.

The shrinkage rules were also the same for consumables, especially food items with a short lifespan. The products have to be proactively sold before their sell by or eat by dates to protect its consumers. Most products have a shelf life and can easily go off if sitting on a shelf for too long. However, as time went on and as systems and businesses became more intellectual, it became evident that there was shrinkage of other kinds and not quite so obvious. Careless damage was possibly the next problem. Mishandling and the dropping or crushing of products had the same effect as theft, rendering products totally unsellable and, therefore, having to be disposed of. Although obvious to a shopkeeper working on his or her own, back in the day, it was just good old common sense and normal business practice with basic accounting skills and ledgers to understand loss at this level. However, as trading grew to the colossal national and even international sizes of today where managers' oversee, sometimes armies of people and with pressure to deliver sales for the shareholders, shrinkage became less obvious and sometimes lost.

It later became understood that shrinkage or erosion had to be carefully managed just as any other product and was, in bigger companies, becoming a sub-industry in itself creating jobs and careers. Auditor roles grew and firms could send in these auditors to investigate where losses were occurring. This is what we call looking after the back door and this means the warehouse or stock room end of our business. We have seen and discussed at length how much hard work and energy goes toward building up staff, sales, standards and service, taking massive amounts of investment, dedication, training and time at the front door or the front of house, customer end of a business. As a manager, learning to manage the back door makes absolute sense on a number of counts. Firstly and most importantly, all your hard work in the business will be shrunk or eroded if you neglect this area after all your efforts to improve the business. Two, it is no good generating lots of money in sales if you and your team are losing it elsewhere, and thirdly, normally as a manager in most sectors our performance will be monitored and measured on our efficiency to cut costs and reduce shrinkage. Potential and glowing careers can be affected by poor control of erosion. One or two poor stocktakes can out trump superb sales results.

Shrinkage Control Measures

In today's computerised world enough is known about shrinkage for it to be targeted, budgeted and compensated for. It is not intended to discuss profit and loss accounts (often referred to as P&Ls) in this book and we have touched on this subject lightly already, but as with all targets and budgets a final, definitive shrinkage figure should be found within these reports. As a retail unit or branch manager we will certainly have access to a set of P&Ls, or as a supervisor we may have access to financial budgets and targets. If this is the case, any company worth its salt will have a budget or target figure (usually expressed as a percentage) for shrinkage. It is most sensible to not only know our sales targets, but our shrinkage targets too. Since profits are hugely affected by shrinkage, any successful manager will always have a clear shrinkage target and reduction plan in tandem with sales. If, due to a specific structure in a company, we do not have access to shrinkage figures, we should ask. If we can ask, we will only show ourselves to be more knowledgeable and more conscientious than previously thought and will only add to our success.

Stock Control

To control this shrinkage problem, it is prudent to know that we are indeed on a diet in the first place. This begins by understanding our business and products and how we and our teams respect our very own stock. We should realise how important it is and handle it with care. This includes all businesses from factory processing or hairdressers' equipment and so on. All around our business is potential waste, potential damage and, of course, potential theft or misuse. Receipts need to be obtained for purchases such as travel, accommodation and fuel so they can be monitored accurately. In the building trade, bags of cements and pots of paint were notorious for being squashed and split. I once had a cash office clerk taking money from the cloth bank bags by unpicking the stitching after we had counted and cashed up and security had sealed them. Unpicking the cloth sack stitching at the bottom, she would remove the bags of coins and then staple up the bottom so they looked unopened with their security tags intact. Shrinkage can come in many forms and it will pay well to get to really understand it. Even being rough handed and disrespectful to our building, property or vehicles means unnecessary cost and repairs, therefore causing shrinkage.

Stocktakes

Shrinkage in its entirety normally reveals itself once a business has taken a stocktake. Here the results and figures can be analysed and compared with previous results or other store results to look for improvement and identify weak spots. Preparing for a stocktake can be a massive and stressful task, but getting it right will reveal true and accurate results with which to move forward. Removing shelves, emptying cupboards and clearing out dead-end corners can relieve a business of thousands of pounds of potential loss. The only true and real way of stocktaking is to physically count it. And that means laying it out for all to see. Only then can an up-to-date and accurate record be made. If we try to massage this result to a more favourable figure it will only roll over to the next stocktake result, giving you a bigger negative result next time. So the best rule is to accept the most current and accurate stocktake, bite the bullet and work on the shrinkage problem the day after your stocktake. Put a shrinkage plan into place as soon as possible and get staff to buy in to it to manage and monitor your shrinkage over the following months until your next stocktake. Not managing your shrinkage is just as bad as knowingly allowing stock to be stolen. Work with your company accountant or auditors and ask them for help and advice. They will understand the facts and figures and help you make sense of it all. Good company auditors are to be there to helpful and point out areas of possible shrinkage rather than apportion blame. Networking with them will help you understand where the problems lie.

Stolen products are always the most obvious, but are not the only form of shrinkage. As we have said, stolen money, small losses or amounts of shortages on deliveries and so on. The list is endless. Perhaps the most obvious and popular or rather unpopular reason for shrinkage is theft. A company has paid all that money to buy or make the product, transport it to its premises and pay staff to place it on the shelves and price it only for it to be stolen. Internal theft by employees is the same shrinkage problem as traditional shoplifting by outsiders and should always be treated as such. As too is the taking of time, tools or equipment. Horror stories of the '70s and '80s told of shipyard and car factory workers in work time, using work tools and materials to manufacture equipment for private use and staff saw no problem with it. Propellers, exhaust pipes, pedals, cranks, fishing weights and so on were all snuck out of the business. Also the friendly, helpful practice of clocking in for absent colleagues. All these actions eroded the businesses operating margins. Clearly this was profit margin shrinkage (or erosion as it also known) at its most visible. Consequently and ironically, then came more shrinkage in the form of strikes in defence of dismissals or redundancies of repeat offenders as companies were blamed for the mistreatment of staff. Here the irony continued as factories and machinery stood idle and dormant for weeks or even months, whilst management and staff sought to find resolutions for these dilemmas. Here the lesson was to understand the workforce's needs, wants and their understanding of the situations, and then be understood by educating the workforce and then passing on and the cementing of information by explaining at length the problems it caused. Real empathy of the damage was never achieved. Empowerment, buy in and ownership with responsibility were not attained. For many large British factory workers, it took decades of constant embarrassment from Japanese companies before we embraced a better work ethic. Eventually British firms had a paradigm shift to get both parties to understand the other side. Management was encouraged to release more information, to empower their teams and give them some ownership so workers felt like they had a stake in what was happening and, in return, malign practices and poor standards slowly ceased through care, trust and responsibility.

As companies became more aware of the shrinkage problem, waste and natural erosion also became more obvious. If we take stock or products off a shelf for display purposes, that product may never be used again and, therefore, shrinks the margin. Here the stock would have to be recorded and logged as display item usage. Taking tiles out of a box and gluing them on a wall, for example, to show off the products would render the tile unsellable or at a very low discounted rate, possibly below cost. Careless waste could be buying more and more tools or equipment for staff when not needed and then carelessly losing or breaking that tool, forcing the purchase of yet more. This too is shrinkage. Companies rarely allow staff to sell below margin, but sometimes as a manager you may sell some-thing off cheaper rather than dispose of it. This too is shrinkage of your profit margin. You may have a great salesperson, but what if you discover they are only great because they sell everything at a discount and some-times at a loss? Refund fraud is also a way to extract money or items from a business, as is using items and then returning them. Having tight management control over our returns and credit systems can also protect our profit margins. The recording of these problems using the 'manage, monitor, measure' formula allows businesses to identify where problems lie and minimise this shrinkage. Instead of making one or two staff redundant to cut costs, why not manage shrinkage tighter to save the same amount of money in the first instance and keep the staff members? The absolute bottom line problem with shrinkage is that it effects our 'bottom line', quite literally. This presents many problems, but mainly a one of cost. Gradually if shrinkage is not controlled within a business or industry, it will eventually add cost to the operation and in the mechanism of economics that cost will be passed on to the consumer and, therefore, dilute the service and expose the industry to be poorly managed.

The politics of commerce historically suggests that the UKs NHS and the old publicly owned British Rail network were the two biggest state-owned offenders of this dilemma during the 1980s era year on year, wasting millions of pounds of taxpayers' money.

Strip Back

Less is more. One can often achieve much more using much less and we as humans tend to over complicate things unnecessarily. As a younger manger, as a trouble shooter often sent in to reorganise troublesome large DIY stores, I would always look for low-hanging fruit and easy picks first. I saw that a lot of our large DIY stores problems often began at the back door, in the warehouses. Sometimes, poor planning of the building or restrictions on yards by councils, or just poor layout often led to over capacity of stock into small warehouses that just couldn't cope with the large vast stock levels needed. Sometimes very successful stores, but with small warehouses would struggle to manage, always struggling to cope with large deliveries to supply the hunger of their growing sales.

Very often was the case of poor exit strategies from old promotions and discontinued ranges. As with most retail businesses holding on to junk supported their stock holding figures and, therefore, embellished bottom line results to shareholders. It is now, as it was back then, in my perception, false accounting. But three million pounds worth of tat, dross and junk that no one wanted still has a monetary weighting on the profit and loss balance sheet of a business and, therefore, the bottom line. Often in these cases there was such a mass of accumulated overstocks, with warehouses bulging at the seams with discontinued stock lines. Directors had failed to make real honest and brutal decisions to cut their losses and clear through discontinued and old seasonal stock lines and the general store managers had simply just lost control of their back door operations. This was often the case and many a store would spend hundreds of man hours, quite literally, running pallets of stock out into backyards and car parks during the day and shipping it all back in at night. This environment was clearly a breeding ground for shrinkage. Stock would be stolen, as one man's junk is another man's treasure (especially if it's free) and shipping stock in and out daily only leads to more damage and loss, even just in time spent doing it. Even as recent as 2010, a well-known national tile company was still doing this in hundreds of stores, shattering and smashing tons of discontinued stock each week as it clattered daily over kerbs and pavements in and out of warehouses into delivery yards. This poorly, underdeveloped area of the business caused large shrinkage problems for many businesses, if not through real loss of stock, then certainly through the loss of man hours wasted continually trying to sort out the problem that it caused. The solution is to strip back and reduce anything, wherever we can. Clear out with a strict target of stripping out anything can reduce time wasted in management of the problem in the first place. Then reduce the problem itself. Remember it doesn't have to be stock as in retail. It could be an excessive cleaning problem caused by others, for example. Cleaners can be stopped from doing their normal cleaning routine because of a larger reoccurring cleaning problem elsewhere. This can be shrinkage and needs to be eradicated to allow normal service to resume.

Shelves Out

One of my policies when I worked in the large multinational retail businesses was to remove the large heavy warehouse shelving that was already in place. Later, for me it became a metaphor and a real example that I used in other areas of management. The less shelving, the better. The less is more theory. Ironically, the warehouse shelving (and/or storeroom space) should hold just enough bestselling and quick-selling lines to prevent running out and, therefore, minimise missed sales opportunities that, of course, leads to maximum sales. To begin the reverse of this paradox, on visiting stores, I would set about removing shelving, causing the managers in charge to deal with and tackle the real problem of getting old junk out of warehouse racking, off warehouse floors and get that stock onto the sales floor areas and sold off. Slowly over time, as I removed more shelves, stores were forced to deal with their stock holding problems and reduce it, which, as discussed, also reduces their shrinkage as damages and lost products are minimised. When discontinued stock and its packaging becomes unfashionable it becomes jaded, ripped and crushed and, of course, it then becomes unmanageable, awkward to handle and stack. The problem becomes exponential and it ceases to be cared for in the same way as fresh stock and eventually, with more shelving added in attempts to curb the problem, it just grows into worse conditions and, of course, the shrinkage grows. As we have discussed, stopping the shrinkage is vital to protecting the business bottom line, so restructuring and organising the 'back door' (warehouse) is key to protecting the overall performance of a business. Therefore, clearing the 'wood from the trees', organising warehouses and training is, I believe, the way forward and removing shelving simply gives the back rooms less space for dead stock, forcing staff to deal with the problems. If you put up a shelf people will always naturally put things on it.

I later used this strategy to deal with normal everyday management and the shelving issue became a metaphor for dealing with everyday work. In/Out trays in offices were a prime example. The less in trays on our desk, the better our performance. I never understood why managers had in, pending, out and haven't a clue trays on their desks. I only ever had one tray. If paperwork was in that tray, clearly it needed to be dealt with. The more filing trays on the desk, the more procrastination and dithering is accomplished and less decisive action taken. This is true of admin offices, documents and duplication, etc. So for me, less really is more. The more you can strip out, strip back and streamline, the more you will speed up and improve efficiency. Overall, the end game is slick, proficiency and a smooth operation as there is clearly less to manage and less to distract. Wherever we can strip out and streamline, we should. We should get rid of any clutter and reduce our shrinkage and losses. At the very most, you will be able to see more clearly where your losses are.

Sheriffs and Supporters

We spoke earlier regarding the need for walking our business on a daily basis. This action also basically acts as policing our business. The constant presence of a manager in and out of staff areas, warehouses and sales floors really does create an impact on not only everyday routines, but on shrinkage too. Managers who show they care and make an effort to come out of their offices can begin to drive down shrinkage in their first day. Looking around the business, with real engagement and talking to our teams, championing the causes and finding staff who are willing to take on projects will immediately put a spin on the routines and practices, thereby protecting and safeguarding our profits. Finding a staff member to sheriff shrinkage for us and take on some responsibility can help immensely, as they can be our eyes and ears. Using SWOT, SMART and SORT analysis approaches and with some team supporters shrinkage can be controlled and reduced to manageable levels.

"The 80-20 rule suggests that 80% of the outcomes can be attributed to 20% of the causes for a given event."

Vilfredo Pareto, Italian engineer and philosopher

"Don't worry where inspiration and creativity comes from, just think about where it can lead."

Anon

Summary

Throughout the Ss, we have not discussed or even mentioned money, marketing departments, advertising budgets or extra sales staff to enhance what we do or what we would wish to do. The aim of the game to success is that we deliver to our customers, bosses, staff and peers real results, but use the resources we have at our disposal. This is the real trick. Using what we already have and by being innovative and creative we can grow sales from humble beginnings. Clearly, if our management role affords us a profit and loss account, we may have some finances available for small quick-win sales initiatives like purchasing banners, for example. However, on the whole the aim here is to use what we have first and prove to senior management that we have used everything in our toolbox to generate the said sales. Of course, once we have demonstrated that we have fully deployed all our skills and resources, we may then feel confident to request some extra spending from head office, marketing or indeed our bank manager!

Throughout the book, we focus our attention on us and what we can achieve for our own success. Understanding ourselves and our teams better will give us much more success and more positive sales will only enhance and reaffirm this. We do not have to spend vast amounts of money to get the basics right. We do not need millions of pounds to get the staff selling and the business pumping. What we do need is a better understanding of the whole jigsaw, some consistency and the courage of our own convictions to make the right choices.

Before we look at our seventh and final S, it is perhaps a good time to reflect and summarise the six Ss discussed already and review them as an overview. The Ss discussed fall naturally into two groups and reveal a methodical and systematic approach to arriving at our final S to success.

Group One, Input

This is what I call the human input group. The self, staff and standards. This is the people or the cognitive group. This group should always take priority over group two as here we are always dealing with people and emotions. We have explored group one at length, our *self*, our staff and our standards, and agree that they surely come first due to them being positively human. These subjects of human activity cannot operate without the other and are the building blocks of all we aim to achieve and rely solely on each other. By bringing them together, as in life, we begin to create societies and places where we can see some form of semblance with law, order and structure, which becomes a safe place in which to operate. We obviously need to organise, sort and manage the Group One things first, so every morning before and on our way to work we should have some positive thoughts, firstly for ourselves, then on how we fully intend to engage and interact with our staff, giving them the same attention and positive energy that we ourselves enjoy. This will grow and improve our standards across the board.

Group Two, Input

This is the production input group with which we busy ourselves daily. Stock, sales and shrinkage. This second group is the doing group or the physical group and the reason we go to work each day. This is where the fruits of our labour are seen and felt. Here in Group Two we roll up our sleeves and get our hands dirty. Group Two relies solely on Group One and cannot perform or operate without it; however, clearly we cannot operate without Group Two as these are the things that deliver our sales results. This is where we measure our economies and growth and, therefore, our successes. Group Two dominates our daily activities and demands so much of our time, but is necessary for output. Group two is how we get to where we wish to be and is the vehicle to our objectives and ultimately the vehicle to our success.

Group Three, Output

Finally we arrive at our outcome group. Our ultimate goal to achieving success is by bringing both input Groups One and Two together and measuring our output. We can label this success as service. This service is the acid test and can be easily measured, as we have with all six headings already. We have discussed these elements at length and agree that the measurements put in place can ensure that standards and parameters can be achieved. This leaves us with the measurement of service. This will be a measurement of our success gained from all previous six elements and will be gauged by feedback from customer-driven opinions or perceptions. This will be a view of how good we are or our brand are, be they a supporter or detractor. Service is the end game of all our work and measured based on a variety of performances. How good our service is depends on how thorough we have been with our efforts of input. How much hard work, dedication and attention to detail we have put in. Providing 'a level' of service will evolve naturally from our endeavours and, as the saying goes, we only get out what we put in.

As we have discussed, service is not merely a smile or a 'come back now, ya all' statement at the checkout. As we now understand it is the end result of a series of many things. It is a product in itself with many, many moving parts. Service is not what the TV ads would have us believe. They are only ambitions and aspirations we can only hope to achieve. Being friendly and polite alone does not deliver 'world-class service'. A smile and wave does not give what the customer wanted in the first instance. These are merely support mechanisms from highly motivated, trained and well-looked-after staff. Delivery of the product or service on time, every time, consistently, without fail is the first and foremost service priority, coupled with the fringe benefits of 'nothing is too much trouble'. If we really value our customers from our input of Groups One and Two we will reap our rewards, judged from the output and indeed the loyalty of our clients who refuse to go elsewhere. This loyalty will be a trust and understanding of our operations leaders (department, branch or sales manager) and our branding, coupled with the high investment we offer in human resources, employed to deliver on a promise over and over, without fail.

"Time is precious, waste it wisely."

T Bromberg

"Good leaders carry their own weather with them."

Chapter 7
Service

Customer Service

Since the dawn of trading we have strived to find an edge over our competitors. Trading has always been competitive. As villages grew so too did the skills and trades. Farmer numbers increased, as did blacksmiths, carpenters and wheelwrights. This clearly caused competition and since then trade has always looked for an advantage over its rivals. The last century and certainly last few decades has seen a marked uplift in service standards driven in the main by advancements in education and technology. Embracing technology allows business and the economy to move forward and create new milestones.

Since around 3000 BC, given all these decades and centuries of innovation and technology, humans once again figured out the best way to trade. It was evident that, for almost for free or with minimum investment, the cheapest and most effective system to grow sales and maintain customer loyalty was the oldest and most tried and tested method available, good old customer service. Once customer service was identified again as a means to an end it wasn't long before firms realised that the looking after customers using specifically trained staff would pay dividends. Americans especially noted this in the '80s and '90s. Household names such as Disneyworld and the likes of Wal-Mart and McDonalds became synonymous for it. 'Queue busters' and 'double baggers' became bywords for great service. Here in the UK, we followed suit, recognising that maximising profits did not have to cost any more money at all. All companies had to do was to get their staff and teams to be happier, friendlier, smile more and be more enthusiastic and helpful, actively identify where their next sales and, of course, wages were coming from. And so it was declared, "The customer is king!"

Identifying the problem was easy. Good old-fashioned, pleasant and helpful service had huge rewards, but sadly changing habits would be the hard part. An education programme was needed to change perceptions and even cultures. Unaware, manufacturers, supermarkets and the public were changing our shopping culture and initially workers seemed reluctant to change and refused to adopt 'the American service culture'. Companies went to great lengths and great cost to drive home the message and the customer service that we are now so used to eventually arrived. The culture of the customer is king, the customer pays our wages and the customer is always right slowly dripped its way through into our psych and into our way of life.

Service Milestones

Looking back, we can reflect with a brief overview of some of the milestones attributed to customer service.

In **1760–1820** the Industrial Revolution created the concept of 'scale' and the need for customer service teams. In **1776** Adam Smith published *The Wealth of Nations*, establishing the basic ideas of competition in the marketplace. In **1868** Watkins Liniment became the first recorded company to offer a money back guarantee. In **1876** Alexander Graham Bell patented the electric telephone. This allowed customer service to take a leap forward as customers could avoid having to travel long distances for product information or to arrange for business meetings or repairs. In **1887,** to encourage sales, Coca-Cola issued the first discount coupon. In **1946** The International Organization for Standards formed in Geneva, Switzerland and in **1965** IBMs MIT CTSS Mail becomes the first host-based electronic mail programme. Later it become email, which became the primary way of interacting with customers online when the web emerged in the 1990s. In the **1960s** private automated business exchanges (PABX) began to be used to handle large numbers of telephone calls. These became the 'call centres' we are more familiar with now, where a large number of operators handle customer enquiries in one location. In 1973 IBM released its 3660 real-time in-store electronic point of sale (barcode) computer system and was installed into Pathmark supermarket store, New Jersey. In 1974 Brubeck Associates built the Intel 8008 cash register systems for McDonald's restaurants.

In the early 1980s the invention of interactive voice response (the thing that lets you say 'yes' or your post-code to the telephone and automatically connects you). In 1980s database software, which would evolve into customer relationship management (CRM) software, evolved to be used in customer service. In 1983 the term 'call centre' was created. Again in the 1980s the help desk emerged to deal with a host of new (<floppy> Disk Operated Systems) DOS-wielding office workers. By around the year 2000 these had evolved into the 'service desk' concept that could help users with the integration of all of their business technology, though the term 'help desk' still is applied. Moving into the late 1980s Sir Clive Sinclair introduced Quantum Link On-Line Messages (OLM) for the Commodore 64, paving the way for instant messaging and later, live chat. Q-Link later became AOL. In 1989 Sir Tim Berner Lee invented the worldwide web and, in the early 1990s, Computer Telephony Integration (CTI), worked with IVR technology to collect information about customer behaviour in telephone systems. The rest, they say, is history as all these amazing inventions catapulted our understanding of service into the 21st century.

Also during the early '70s UK ITV (independent television networks) usage was growing rapidly, allowing people to see other worlds and lives, allowing the public to compare. Companies quickly jumped on this technological bandwagon to promote their wares and drive sales, advertising great offers and promotions. Private businessmen were now able to purchase previously government-owned airlines and promote romantic travel with impeccable, glamorous service. In the '90s service gurus popped up all over, in paperbacks, on VHS videos and on cassette tapes. Service management itself was becoming a booming industry, offering a host of advice and guidance on how to woo new clients and retain old ones. The words 'world-class service' were starting to be used and the newly privatised British Airways airline was marked as the consummate standard of world-class service. With the digital dawn arriving, companies began to harness huge amounts of information and knowledge, giving them the edge over their competitors. Local borough councils began using CRM (customer relations management) systems. These systems were being installed all over the UK and these computers collated information, allowing one operator to answer many different customer requests and thereby improving their telephone service. Soon these borough councils held masses of detailed information and data on their residents and communities, including electoral lists, which were all vigorously sold to the highest bidder.

Then in the early 1990s people began to use the internet. You may have heard of it? In 1992 Customer Service Week was established as the first week in October by President George HW Bush. Mid-1990s the CRM as we know it began to grow, led by software company Gartner, though many others also competed. As a result of more sophisticated customer data tracking, more companies began providing gifts for customer loyalty, such as cash back on credit cards, frequent-flier miles and discounts for multiple purchases. In 1998 Jeremy Miller invented Jabber/XMPP, the open-source technology that most live chat is built on. In the late 1990s and early 2000s outsourcing customer service to offshore locations gained popularity with companies as the dotcom bust occurred and businesses looked to cut costs. However, as we moved on into the noughties (2000 - 2009) companies turned away from offshore customer service centres as customers felt alienated by agents with whom they could not relate and through poor language failings struggled to have empathy with Western clients. Language barriers and script reading became its demise. In 1999 Salesforce.com launched and grows to be the global leader in CRM. In the mid-2000s the rise of the online help desk came with the launch of Zendesk, Freshdesk, Zoho, Desk.com and others. In 2006 Twitter launched. You may have heard of that too? By 2011 65 million tweets were sent each day and companies began to find Twitter a good platform to respond to customers quickly when they have issues (or compliments) and to have a sense of the person's 'social relevance' based on number of followers.

We can see, from all these inventions plus improvements in manufacturing processes that over the decades service demand grew and grew. Suppliers, manufacturers, agents and retailers realised that, with growing economies at home and booming economies overseas from the likes of Japan and Taiwan, came more and more choice and at cheaper rates. I remember as a child, most toys were made in Hong Kong and then later in Taiwan. Clients and customers could now vote with their feet and shop elsewhere. They were no longer constrained by main-stream manufacturer monopolies. One major indication of a business, or indeed industry, bending to customer demand and forced to improve service was the banking industry. In the older days banks and similar institutions would quite literally close for lunch. Nowadays in a 24-hour, seven-day-a-week world, banks and similar financial business realised that to deliver to their client base a more relevant, up-to-date service, they were forced to acknowledge that customers too needed to do bank business on their lunch breaks. Lunch times needed to be managed to support the constant demand of their customers. This had been, for many years, a common practice in retail businesses. Eventually the increased use of internet (online) banking would reduce staff levels and increase branch closures. But as we have learnt, customer service is only part of our real service story. Real service is much more than all these milestones.

The Seventh S is Service

As we gain a fuller understanding of 'all The Ss' and bring them together to complete the formula, we should by now have a better understanding of what we mean by holistic service. Only once we understand the first six Ss do we really begin to develop a deeper understanding of the meaning of service. Here we do not just mean general customer service in the everyday sense. We will now have a greater understanding that our perception of service is very different to normal everyday customer service. Our understanding of true service now comes from a deeper, more calculated knowledge, research, hard work and preparation with a trail of procedures that naturally leads us to where we want to be. Providing a service that is second to none and industry leading. If we have learnt nothing else, we will know that if a job is worth doing it is worth doing well and if we are going to engage in service, we should do it to its very best outcome. However, 'world-class service' means different things to different people. As we now understand, our staff are all different; therefore, so too are our expectations and excellent service to one can be average to another. Every ad, every TV and glossy magazine image of quality service we see will always reveal images of beautiful models purporting real interest and empathy with a client, but this literally is just the glossy face and not the real hub of it. If the images are to be true and not merely inspirational, how did we get to this image? What actions lead us to this point?

This is because we do not simply rely on or accept that service is just a shallow 'customer service'-based concept. It is much deeper, as we have already established. It goes far beyond a puppy eyed Disneyland smile and a fast-food restaurant uniform complete with baseball cap. Our service approach is an all-encompassing, grass-roots-up approach offering a comprehensive and trustworthy ideology, built on common sense and an honest, professional, hard work ethic. This is our branding. This is how we stamp our name on the service we offer. Look at what we have gone through to deliver it. Look at the toil and trouble we have taken to understand and research it and then support it. Our service is not just decorative bunting and Colgate smiles, or a quick presentation on how we should treat customers. Our idea of service now stands shoulders above the opposition. We can now provide a serious challenge to our competition and provide a superior service that encompasses everything the consumer or client requires. The highest of standards, readily available, well-maintained products or services, ready to go, in a spotless environment, encouraged by a highly enthusiastic, motivated and positive sales and support teams.

Sometimes it's not how we get there; it's the end result that counts. But if we need an end result, we must have a first step and a second step and so on and it is those behind-the-scene steps that deliver the final word. Without the latter it is no good us striving for customer service if our management are not trained or they are not happy or motivated, or your staff are terrible and rude, or our sales or production floor is filthy, strewn with empty packaging and pallets, or our store, factory, shop or dental practice is just too difficult to find. Perhaps the stock we have is poorly displayed, if displayed at all, or maybe damaged, or just unaccounted for and not replenished correctly and constantly out of stock and, therefore, unavailable to the customer. Perhaps our stock is not looked after and is constantly being stolen and again unavailable for sale. None of this is conducive to good service. But service just isn't service if we have not put all the other elements into action. Under these conditions, great customer service may work initially, for a short period, but clients are savvy and will cotton on to what's happening behind the scenes as their demands, needs and wants are constantly undermined.

The complete, holistic service measure is simply what your customer base says it is, not what we think it is. We all have different ideas of what constitutes great service. To younger clients it could be speed of delivery; to older customers it could be attentiveness; to the middle-aged it could be courtesy or politeness. To a busy business entrepreneur it may solely be just good constant delivery of the product or service. To a purist it could be all the above. To many it is reducing the time and effort required of the customer to enable them to solve their problem (as we said, nothing should get in the way of a sale). Some people are married to our brand and require very little input; others are unaware of our brand and need to be persuaded.

Value for Money (VFM)

This is an opinion measurement based on experience used by many older folk who value a product's reliability and longevity. Nowadays many items are made so cheap that they do not last long and younger people may not care so much as long as it has done its job once and got them out of a fix. They may not be bothered about recycling and reusing over and over. Another example is price. Is a 10-pound wristwatch value for money if it lasts the owner years and years with trouble-free service? Yes, it was still cheap at 10 pounds, but it was certainly value for money. Many of us may have fathers who still have tools from their youth or their tradesmen days, indicating the reliability (value for money) of those tools. Reliability makes a big statement in a product, but also in the overall package that we as managers deliver. Our total output is for all our endeavours to be classed as one whole product that delivers time and time again. This reliability too then becomes value for money.

Assurance

Assurance can be measured by the knowledge level, professionalism and politeness of staff and to what effect these skills are put to use. After all the coaching, development, empowerment, trust and responsibility afforded, these skills and qualities should be put to maximum use and managed constantly as a barometer of customer comfort.

Tangibles

These are the things we can see and touch. The car park, our kerb appeal, our building, inside and out. The cleanliness of the shop floor, the clarity of our website the quality of our business cards, equipment and presentation of staff and uniforms.

Empathy

This can be measured by how much our employees care and how much attention our people give to our individual customers. How bothered we are to want to give great service. Do our teams point and nod to things or do we lead our customers to the product and actively suggest options or better fits? Do we really want to solve the customer's problem? If so, how do our teams go about that?

Responsiveness

This can be defined by our willingness to provide a speedy and prompt result with a genuine want to offer quick service. Have you ever stood waiting for staff to finish a conversation about tea breaks before they pick up on your waiting or request? This is most rude and very unprofessional and as managers we should look out for this, as, if unmanaged, this poor practice can easily spread

Mystery Shopper

This is usually where we hire a paid agent or outsider. Under certain guidelines and criteria they will perform genuine customer purchases and refunds in order to experience and feel the whole service provided, then report back to us on the performance of their overall experience.

Surveys

These are generally post-service questionnaire reports conducted from call centres, but can also be in-house straight after the purchase, although evidence suggests more positive responses when the client has been allowed time to reflect on his or her experience.

Recent surveys suggest that 41% of people still use the telephone to complain to a company and 63% of people use email, but a significant proportion (20%) will use social media to air their gripes, with this figure rising to 36% for Generation Y (under 25-year-olds). Of UK business leaders, 83% feel that customers are the biggest driver of change and are the biggest pressure point for businesses today. Of UK businesses, 53% believe that customer service has become more important over the past 12 months. Of UK consumers, 66% believe customer service has either stayed the same or deteriorated over the past three years. Only 3% believe it has improved a lot and 22% a little. Of customers, 81% would be willing to pay more in order to receive superior customer service. Only 29% of the UK's small businesses believe that customer service is a key differentiator in today's competitive marketplaces. This compares to 88% of Spanish businesses and 77% of Italian businesses who see customer service as being the differentiator that helps them stand out: UK businesses lose 21 million customers a year due to long queues. As much as 59% of shoppers are not prepared to wait in a queue, with 18% saying that they would go to an alternative shop, and 32% of frustrated shoppers say they would turn to online retailers! As many as 90% of UK shoppers walk away without buying something if they get bad customer service! Forty-one per cent of shoppers said the biggest frustration is lack of interest in their needs. Fifty-nine per cent of UK shoppers want more staff to recommend products, as it makes the experience more personal, and 80% of shoppers want to be taken to a product when asking its whereabouts. When asked what the key drivers were for a customer to spend more with a company, 40% said improvement in the overall customer experience and 35% said provide quick access to information and make it easier for customers to answer questions. Fifty-seven per cent of customers will wait three seconds or less for a website to load before abandoning it. Seventy-four per cent of customers leave if a website doesn't load on their smartphone in five seconds. In fact, a one-second delay in load time would cost Amazon an estimated $1.6 billion a year! Rude staff are the most common reason for poor customer service by more than 50% of UK customers, followed by timeliness (19%) and the inability to fix a customer's reported problems (19%). The top five reasons that create a decrease in customer loyalty are: being transferred between staff; no response to an email; length of time on hold; being unable to reach a human and unknowledgeable staff. It is estimated that seventy-one per cent of customers go online first whenever they have a problem with a product, forty-nine per cent of customers wanting help from a company's customer service team contact them by email and 43% pick up the phone! Fifty-one per cent of people who make a complaint online expect a response, but 85% of those questioned have never received one! Eighty-five per cent of customers said they were delighted (27%) or very/somewhat happy (58%) on receiving a public response to their comments on social media from a brand. Forty-six per cent of customers aged 24 and below use social media to air their grievances; 33% of them say that responses are too slow. Ninety-one per cent of customers don't always complain when they receive poor customer service, with more than 40% of them thinking it is not worth complaining, as accompanies simply don't care! Only 27% of customers said they either always or often give feedback when they've had great customer service! Eighty-one per cent of customers would be more likely to give feedback if they knew there would be an instant response! When asked what is most likely to keep them loyal, UK customers responded:

Improved trust in the business (3.1%) – Outstanding reputation of the business (4.9%) – Good loyalty rewards (17.1%) – Cost (17.3%) – Excellent customer service (27.5%) – Quality of product or service (30.2%). Eighty-six per cent of customers are more likely to purchase something following a good customer experience and 64% are unlikely to repurchase something if they are very dissatisfied with the customer service interaction. Forty-eight per cent of internet users told other people 'all the time' about a good customer service experience with a company. Seventy-eight per cent of online customers recommend a brand to friends and other contacts after a great customer experience and 68% reported that they spend more money on the company's items. And finally here's a 'bonus' 26th statistic (that is a customer delight!)... more than 65% of UK bosses believe that businesses can't keep up with the pace of change in today's competitive markets and 57% agree that an inability to respond rapidly and effectively to change is one of the most significant risks their business faces today.

Social Media

The use of media is a great vehicle to collate and gather measurements of service by asking clients to comment, like or subscribe to your postings, thereby increasing traffic flow or exposure to websites and blogs, etc. This digital approach is normally very accurate and often reflects a very true presentation. Google and Facebook now profile their users' replies and their responses so accurately that future advertising can now be tailored 100% accurate to suit the client even to the point of their voting habits!

Loyalty Ladder and Repeat Customer

This is usually a physical count of how many times a customer has used our service or bought our products and where that customer is on the ladder of loyalty. Are they fairly new to our products or services, therefore trialling us, or are they lifetime users and, therefore, absolute advocates? Do they shop with us because their parents did and will they recommend us to others?

Store Cards

This is possibly the most accurate and reflective method of measuring customers' repeat business and, therefore, their loyalty. The cards carry many personal details of the client and can even measure demographics, shopping times and even peculiar purchase habits and frequency. Passcard is believed to be the first type of loyalty card to be used, created around 1981 by Gary Wilson, and the concept is believed to be taken up by Sainsbury's home improvements arm, Homebase. The scheme was launched as the Spend and Save Scheme, awarding points to the card for pounds spent.

Brand insistence	Advocate
Repeat Purchases	Client
Trialist	Customer
Not Yet Purchased	Prospect

The Loyalty Ladder

Synergy

The Oxford Dictionary suggests that synergy be defined as 'the interaction or cooperation of two or more organisations, substances, or other agents to produce a combined effect greater than the sum of their separate effects'. Put simply, one plus one equals three, or four or even five. "The whole is greater than the sum of its parts." This is exactly how we project our service within the Seven Ss. The synergy we get from combining the six skills from the two groups is huge, as the output is far more than we had hoped for. Synergy is not harmony. Our two groups do indeed work together in harmony and sit beside each other and rely on each other, but for us Group One plus Group Two equals far more, making Group Three, service, so much more than we expected, allowing us to deliver high-quality, top-class and even world-class, market-leading service.

Service Journey

We all understand and know what service is, right? Well, we possibly all think we are all experts in this field. As consumers we are all receivers of this well-tried and tested act; however, service is not just the human physical act of saying hello and goodbye politely, although it is certainly a huge part of the customer experience. But it really is much more than that. As we have seen already, it is the sum of all the other Ss. All the other activities and endeavours. It really is the fruit of all our labour and if we get the sums right it is the cheapest, most cost-effective way of growing our business. If we understand the very essence and core of service and get it right consistently, we will finally experience true service. When we understand all this and deliver on it consistently, we can confidently measure, accurately, our success. Combining our efforts in self, staff and standards with stock, sales and shrinkage, we will ultimately deliver on true service. As we have seen, service is not just about a smile and a thank you. Great service comes from good-quality stock being ordered correctly in appropriate quantity and with appropriate standards maintained. Service in our context comes from a passionate desire to improve oneself and one's own standards and to drive this ethos through into our teams. This is perhaps the Holy Grail and ultimate success of being a successful manager.

Sales Journey

Before we look at using standards for personal branding, let us first look at standards to help us see the complete picture. As managers we are all engaged in commercial activities to drive a sale, win attention to our department or win a government grant or just to gain recognition of performance. To do this we rely on the standard of the *customer journey*, the person, customer or the body we wish to attract. As with nature, survival and evolution, the standards to win must be high. The bowerbird builds intricate nests and bright corridors to attract the very best females. He knows the best bachelor pad wins the day! Only the biggest and strongest lion will get to mate with the pride and so, the best business gets the contract. But winning is an end result of a journey. The *customer journey*. For a business it is a survival journey. The service journey is the same as the sales journey. This is also referred to as the customer journey. As we have seen, for most customers the journey may start with a TV commercial or a leaflet posted through their door. This commercial or leaflet has to be good enough to stand out from all the other messages. The ad has to wow and, therefore, has to be of high standard. So here it pays to invest, research and get it right, first time. The ad campaign could be the very first engaging connection with the customer and so, the journey begins. You have impressed the potential client with your high standard of advertising; now, for the customer, the next step will be to make contact. This may be through your website, call centre or premises. The benchmark has been set and the standard will now be expected. The next step of the customer journey must match or better the TV or leaflet ad. If your call centre operates to an inferior standard with long ring or on hold times or your website was thrown together quickly and is difficult to load up or navigate, the *customer journey* can finish here. How many of us have searched for holidays on a laptop and soon moved on to another firms' sites as the earlier one was just too slow to load up the deals? The standard has to match the previous step. Assuming our backwater restaurant website was enjoyable and the telephone was answered promptly and professionally, the journey may continue on to the next phase. Remember, the point being stressed here is that high standards across the board count. For the client, a drive by or a visit may now be imminent and, as we said before, if the house-keeping, maintenance or hygiene of the place does not look good, it can be game over for many businesses. At any point in the journey if the standards aren't there, the potential client will easily become switched off.

Service Alternatives

We mentioned earlier that it may be that as managers our work or industry does not deal with the public directly. We may work providing services to private clinics or care homes, education, mental health or manufacturing. The rules still apply and I strongly suggest that all seven rules, especially service, still prevail. You may wonder where or how the service output can be applied, but earlier in the book we discussed that service is not a one-way street and this is the alternative service offer, as it is not service in the 'customer service' sense. We still have a job to do and, therefore, using the Seven Ss, we should still always look to deliver great service to our peers, our staff, our line mangers and, of course, the company we work for. Service in this context simply

The Segments and Cycle of The Seven Ss

means outstanding performance and if we are capable of it we should strive to deliver it over and over again, consistently, to ultimately achieve the success we desire. Staff, colleagues and mangers have a right to expect great service from us also and here it can be measured as professional performance and conduct.

Now we can see how the cycle is perpetual and never-ending. We can see now, it does not matter where we start the process, as we acknowledge that we must start somewhere and that self is probably the best place. We should now have a better understanding that our main goal for complete success is service; however, we will also have a better understanding that service is not simply a smile, a wink and a wave goodbye.

As with the Greeks, the first real known civilisation and functioning society, they clearly understood a form of Maslow's hierarchy and their legacy or brand was democracy (their service output). This was built on and relied on huge pillars of immoveable concepts. This branding still lasts today thousands of years after it was first realised. Rising up, as the famous citadel of Acropolis, to support their legacy (their service) or brand (their democracy), the Greek pillars of strength were social, political, philosophical, scientific, art and literature. And just like the Greeks, we should by now understand that great service and world-class service, our seventh S, can only be achieved from a deep-rooted psych, like the stones of the Acropolis, resting on top of the six pillars that rise up from the deep foundations we have built on. It is only from the strength and accurate conception of our six pillars that we are able to lay the final cross member stone of service.

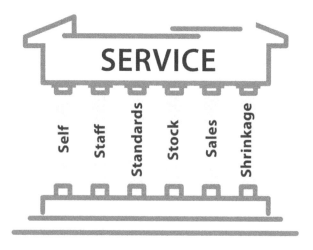

The Six Pillars of Service

Food for Thought

I suggest the formula of the Seven Ss are not only commercial management tools. They succeed daily in the private and domestic world too. Once understood, the Seven Ss can be applied to our private lives also, to help us all improve our relationships. My parents' goals, objectives and ambitions in life were far more modest than many families of today. For many parents back then the rule was just to get by and do the very best for themselves and their kids. Unaware of the formula, I believe my parents embraced the Seven Ss and dealt nobly with self (themselves), the staff (us, their kids) and then they worked on standards by the way they brought us up and what went on in and outside the home. They worked hard on stock, ensuring we had everything we needed, from clothes to food to education. Sales were the good times, the sad times, the happy occasions, the fun and memories created and shrinkage was both the careful management of the family finances as well as maintaining our health and well-being. Every penny was looked after and spent wisely. Waste of any kind was not tolerated, including switching off TVs and lights as soon as we had finished using them. Shrinkage could also be seen as maintaining their standards for us and under great hardships and financial pressure not allowing their morals or standards to slip. Also perhaps the gap between what they ultimately had hoped for and what they actually got, both for themselves and for us, the children. To get a true value on that we would probably have to ask them. Finally, to the output, the service. This was the overall love and attention and quality parenting we got and how we feel about that even to this day. This is their legacy, their branding. Looking back, Mum and Dad did a great job, I reckon, and by anyone's standards they were very successful. Although they did not know it, they applied all the Seven Ss well. Job done; mission accomplished.

Final Word

As I mentioned at the beginning, this book seeks merely to act as a guide in steering the reader or learner through the basic formalities of management and managing. The Seven Ss are to serve as a gentle daily reminder to simply touch on each of the seven subjects or headings every day. By giving each heading some of your time every day, you will dramatically reduce the risk of that old evil management circus trick, of poor plate spinning. The art of poor plate spinning sees us frantically running around back and forth, desperately attempting to keep all seven plates up, and spinning them wildly on their sticks whilst we run from one end of the stage (business) to the other. In fact, following the Seven Ss rule will only enhance one's skills and help the reader positively develop the art of plate spinning to a high performance.

As I close off the completion of this book and we pass through New Year's Eve into a new year, I reflect and look back at my successes, historically and more recent. On reflection, we can all measure our own success and identify where we can improve, where we want to improve and how we can improve. As we raise our glasses to toast new successes of the future, whilst doing so it is important to remember that it is not what we do on New Year's Eve that is significant or important. Our actions of a one-night event are purely symbolic gestures

shared with friends and family. Life, as with any business, simply goes on and needs to be managed. Our
festive actions are just that. Symbolic gestures to the
passing of time and the celebration of another milestone.
It is not how we celebrate the arrival of the New Year,
but what we do as individuals and as managers on the
very first day of the New Year and the days after that
are important.

SELF strong surprising splendid
splendiferous **structure** *success* self-worth self-discipline
sell **STAFF** sight sound smell senses smart
sixfold seize **suffix** sequence **simultaneous**
swanky **STANDARDS** supply spectacular
steady **sufficient** succinct *sociable* SIMPLY
sumptuous smile sweetness sacred superior
swift special safety special **STOCK** synergy
satisfied self-esteem soulful secure satisfied
SERENDIPITOUS SERVICE LEVELS surrogate
solutions systematic synergy support stealth
synonymous **SALES** Symbolise **scented**
salubrious sacred satisfaction salvation
SHRINKAGE saintly scrumptious seamless
SELFLESS sensational superb sensuous
sensible significant **SKILLED** smooth
sophisticated stretching spontaneous swift speedy
sportsmanlike stable **SERVICE** sensibility

About the Author

After several years of active service in the Armed Forces, from the early nineties onward the author has worked for some of the UK's largest PLC companies.

Sponsored by an employer, he studied at Manchester Metropolitan University where his degree thesis work assisted in a cultural directional shift for one of the largest retailers in the UK at the time. He introduced accredited NVQ learning into a well-known national company and also developed a Manager and Assistant Manager training and development programme for another household name PLC.

He went on to establish his own group of companies and later took on teaching certificates and added to his repertoire, Certified Apprenticeship Assessor.

He has lectured at the University of Cumbria and Furness College and is founder of Ha-Lo Solutions and Ha-Lo Consultants Ltd.

After returning to the UK, he now lectures locally and runs his own business. He currently freelances his work to local businesses and schools and also works at a Cumbria school for young persons on the autistic spectrum.

9 781839 750298